KLAUS ST. RAINER

# COCKTAILS

### THE ART
### OF MIXING
### PERFECT DRINKS

# CONTENTS

# PREFACE

Coming, sir! I have been working in bars and hotels for almost 25 years and in 2010 I was given the opportunity to take over the Golden Bar in Munich, along with my partner Leonie von Carnap. During this time I've managed to acquire a fair bit of experience. Highlights certainly include the five years I spent as a bar manager with Ernst Lechthaler in his international bar-catering outlets from Los Angeles to Dubai, as well as the subsequent seven years I spent fine-tuning my skills in Schumann's bar in Munich.

From behind the world's bar counters I have witnessed not only the bleakest of times for the cocktail, but also the dawn of a new golden cocktail era at the end of the 1990s. This has had a formative impact on my own style, as have my travels to source the products I work with and my countless books. From the sugar fields of Mexico, to Scotland's single malt distilleries and the coffee roasters in Australia, I travel the world in search of new experiences and ideas.

Now I'm putting this knowledge into practice at the Golden Bar. The Golden Bar was opened in 1937 in the Haus der Kunst (House of Art) in Munich. After the war, the gilded interiors with their global drinks-themed facades disappeared behind whitewashed walls. These rooms, steeped in history, were "rediscovered" in 2003, and creatively and conscientiously re-interpreted, introducing new ideas – and that is exactly how I deal with the drinks in this book. Most are based on classics, which I transform with the help of modern concepts and technology.

My philosophy throughout is quite simple: never accept anything but the best. I have always resisted working with products that don't live up to my idea of quality. A drink is the sum of its ingredients – which is something always to keep in mind. All the drinks you see in the photos were produced with the listed ingredients and photographed in the Golden Bar. Furthermore, the glasses and utensils used are sometimes originals that are up to 200 years old.

Finally, amid all this creativity I have never forgotten the importance of excellent customer service, which as bartenders we must provide day in and day out. Only once you have gained your customer's complete trust can you fulfil your mission as a true cocktail evangelist.

CHEERS

KLAUS ST. RAINER

# CLASSIC DRINKS ARE FUN!

Many drinks that we consider to be classics today have been copied constantly and modified over time. So the modern mixing style "classics with a twist", which has been ubiquitous for a while now, is really just as old as the story of cocktails itself. The "twist" is typical of my style, but as far as possible I always try to preserve the connection to the original classic.

## THE NEW GOLDEN AGE OF THE COCKTAIL

Since the late 1990s, a great deal has changed in bars across the world. Prior to this period, drinks were mixed with too much juice and syrup and many classics were still interpreted incorrectly. For example, thanks to prohibition the American whisky in classics such as the Manhattan was replaced by (originally smuggled) Canadian whisky. It took until the turn of the century for this bad habit to die out. Of course, drinks have also altered naturally over the course of time; for instance, the Dry Martini (see p.76), which began as a harmonious combination of gin, plenty of vermouth, bitters, and the fragrant aroma of lemon zest, has gradually evolved into a plain old glass of schnapps with an olive.

Classic drinks were originally creations that had been carefully thought through. In the 19th century, bartenders had to be truly resourceful due to often poor-quality spirits and a dearth of exotic ingredients. If no citrus fruits were available, as recently as 150 years ago syrups would have been boiled down from vinegar, sugar, and other fruits to impart acidity to a drink. Using good-quality ingredients and simple techniques to achieve optimal results should still be paramount today. This requires knowledge and skill: something every bartender should possess and which I'll gladly share with you here.

Today we are experiencing another golden age of the cocktail. The abundance of products available makes it far easier to be creative. In the past, good-quality mint would have been available only from June until the end of August. Nowadays, products from all over the world are available year round, from Japanese cask-aged soy sauce to prized batches of mezcal from Mexico.

In addition, there are the technical innovations. Inexpensive sous vide equipment is available (see p.158) to produce syrups and infusions, and everyday dehydrating devices mutate into dehydrators for the production of cocktail "chips" and highly aromatic powders or dusts (see p.162). The textures of ingredients can be easily altered, too. A good example of this is the Blood and Sand (see p.128) in which I remove the orange juice from the original recipe and transform it into a light foam with the help of some xanthan and a whipping syphon (see p.162). As you drink, the bitter foam tickles the lips, while the strongly aromatic beverage glides over the palate. The ingredients are the same as in the original recipe, but it is a completely new drinking sensation.

For several years now, the "cuisine" style has also been very popular. This approach involves the use of products and techniques more typical in a kitchen than in a bar. A whole variety of herbs and vegetables, even meat and ham, find their way into new recipes. The Bloody Geisha (see p.116) or the Toxic Garden (see p.56) both belong to the realm of cuisine-style cocktails.

## ABOUT THIS BOOK

For a decent home bar you will need a good range of basic spirits (see pp.15–16), which you can eventually expand on, adding drinks catalogued in the Alcohol ABC (see pp.164–167). Many of recipes in the book can be mixed up using just a few basic spirits. You can make nearly all the additional ingredients yourself by trying out the basic recipes in the Appendix (see pp.158–163). Alternatively, of course, you can always fall back on recommended ready-made products, but if you have time, always opt for home-made ingredients. From the home-made ginger beer alone (see p.42), a whole array of exquisite drinks can be made that will cause a sensation among your guests. It's well worth the effort!

The drinks are divided into three chapters. In the first and second chapters, you will learn how to produce delicious results with little experience. In the third chapter, you can learn how to go freestyle for special occasions and evening events, something, with a bit of practice, you really should try. In the Appendix (see pp.172–173) you can search for the perfect drink according to your mood or situation.

On page 14, you will find a key to the symbols used in the book. Whether you are looking for a strong, warm drink for the evening, non-alcoholic cocktails, or easy-to-prepare recipes for evenings with lots of guests, you can use the symbols to guide you. On page 24 you will find out about bottled drinks that can be prepared easily in advance, for example, for parties.

Finally, a bit of sound advice: it is of course important to treat alcohol responsibly. Crossing the boundary into alcoholism is easier than one might imagine, and then things are not remotely funny. Some drinks in this book are very strong, which is why you should drink water alongside them. I prefer to recommend fewer, albeit stronger, drinks, than an abundance of "chi chi" drinks that are easily quaffable, but in the end are sure to give you a headache because they contain so much sugar. The same applies to quality: it is far better to indulge a bit less, but of the highest quality, and savour with true passion.

So now it's time to get started. I wish you all plenty of fun mixing and imbibing!

# EQUIPMENT

Using the right equipment for mixing is just as important as having top-notch ingredients. To begin, you don't need much more than a shaker, mixing glass, and a strainer. If you want to delve in a bit deeper, you should consider acquiring a dehydrator or cold dripper (see p.12).

### SHAKER

This is used for the preparation of shaken drinks. One variety is the Boston shaker, which consists of a glass section with a metal section that fits over it. Alternatively, you can use two-piece metal shakers and three-piece shakers, which usually have an integral sieve underneath the cover flap that saves you having to use a strainer. The latter, however, are best suited to drinks with clear ingredients. The best options are shakers that are completely metal, or shakers made from precious metals, because drinks created in these will be noticeably colder (see p.13, picture 13).

### MIXING GLASS

This is a large glass with a pouring lip in which all stirred drinks are prepared (see p.13, picture 13).

### STRAINER

A bar strainer with a spiral is called a Hawthorne strainer. This fits perfectly onto a Boston shaker or a two-piece metal shaker. A one-piece bar strainer without the spiral is called a julep strainer. The julep strainer fits particularly well into most mixing glasses. Both varieties (picture 1) are used to strain ice from a drink.

### TEA STRAINER

A small tea strainer (picture 2) can be held between the strainer and the glass to strain out fine pieces of ice or fruit.

### BAR SPOON

This is used for stirring drinks, as a bar measure (1 bsp = 5ml), and the flat end can be used to crush small, not too hard ingredients such as sugar cubes (picture 3).

### MEASURING CUP

You can use this to start with to mix up the recipes correctly (picture 4), although you should also train yourself to pour without one. Practise with water, pouring it out and then checking your measure afterwards. Soon you'll be pretty confident, and working without using a measuring beaker looks far more impressive.

### TONGS

You can use tongs to move individual ice cubes, sugar cubes, or fruit decorations hygienically and elegantly. My favourites are the large tweezer tongs (picture 5) or metal chopsticks (picture 6).

### ICE PICK AND ICE SCOOP

You will need an ice pick to knock large chunks and (with a bit of practice) ice cubes out of a block of ice. For reasons of hygiene, the ice scoop shouldn't be left lying on the ice after use (see p.11, picture 7).

### KNIFE

A sharp knife is needed for lots of bar tasks, from cutting up fruit to carving out shapes from ice. I have a preference for small, Japanese knives, such as the Global brand (see p.11, picture 8).

### MUDDLER

A professional muddler or a 30cm (12in) long wooden pestle is used for mashing or muddling fruits and for crushing ice (see p.11, picture 9).

### ATOMISER

To imbue glasses with a particular aroma, you simply fill a little scent bottle with the desired ingredient and moisten the glass from the inside using the spray (see p.11, picture 10).

### FINE GRATER

This is used for grating ingredients such as nutmeg or lemon zest (see p.11, picture 11).

### LEMON SQUEEZER

Pressing by hand will produce the best juice. For small citrus fruits the so-called elbow press is recommended (see p.11, picture 12). For larger fruit, a free-standing juicer is easier to handle. Even the traditional juicers, where you twist the halved fruit on a ridged cone, give excellent results. For larger quantities of juice, you can also use an electronic juicer.

### JUICERS

An electronic juicer (centrifuge) is indispensable for producing juices from ingredients that can't be pressed, such as apple, pineapple, or ginger.

### ELECTRIC MIXER

This is used for creating frozen drinks (see p.82), for preparing foams (see p.162), or for grinding spices.

### WHIPPING SYPHON AND SODA SYPHON

A whipping syphon is useful, for example, to produce fresh syrup quickly (see p.158). I also use it for sophisticated foams (see p.162). A soda syphon aids the carbonisation (the addition of carbon dioxide) of lemonades and other beverages (picture 15).

### COLD DRIP

A cold dripper is a Japanese coffee machine for making cold brew coffee. In this method, (iced) water drips slowly through the filter (picture 14). The result is highly aromatic and contains very few bitter compounds. The machine is also ideally suited for preparing tea and above all for creating alcoholic macerations (see p.163). My favourite is the brand Hario.

### DEHYDRATOR

A simple inexpensive dehydrator (picture 16) helps facilitate the production of "dusts" (see p.162) as well as ham and fruit "chips". Alternatively, you can use the oven.

# GLASSES

**GLASSES
SMALL BEAKER**

**WINE GLASS**

**HIGHBALL**

**COCKTAIL GLASS**

**LONG DRINK GLASS**

**TEA CUP**

**CHAMPAGNE FLUTE**

**OLD FASHIONED GLASS
OR TUMBLER**

**SILVER POT
AND SMALL CUP**

**PUNCH BOWL**

**SILVER GOBLET**

**ABBREVIATIONS IN THE BOOK**
bsp = bar spoon, tbsp = tablespoon,
tsp = teaspoon, dash = spritz

• • •
**FOR LOTS OF GUESTS**

ϟϟϟ
**WARM**

—
**NON-ALCOHOLIC**

# BASIC ALCOHOLIC INGREDIENTS

The following alcoholic beverages should be stocked in every bar. You'll find additional recommendations in the "Alcohol ABC" (see pp.164–167).

### BITTERS

Bitters are a bartender's salt. There's barely a classic cocktail that can get by without them. And in modern mixology, too, bitters are often what smooth off the final raw edges. I often use two of my own brands: Sexy Bitters (spicy, warm, and strong) and OK Drops (floral aromas, camomile, chocolate), both of which are available internationally (see p.174). In place of Sexy Bitters you could also use Angostura Bitters or home-made aromatic bitters (see basic recipe on p.156). All other bitters are listed in the Appendix (see p.164).

### CHAMPAGNES

Champagnes for mixing should always be dry and of a sufficiently high quality that you would also be happy to drink them straight. Cheap champagnes or their substitutes will provide no pleasure. My recommendations are Perrier Jouët Grand Brut, Bollinger Special Cuvée Brut, or Jaquesson.

### GIN

When all sorts of herbs and botanicals are surrounded by juniper and infused in a neutral alcohol before the whole thing is subsequently distilled, we are talking about gin; and if no flavours or sugar are added, the result is a London dry gin, a location independent quality label for top-quality gin. If delicate flavours are added this is called distilled gin. My favourite for a crisp gin and tonic and for mixing is Tanqueray No. Ten, which adds a robust backbone to all beverages with its citrus fruit flavours and 47.3% abv (alcohol by volume).

### RUM

Rum is a spirit that is fermented and distilled from sugar cane juice or molasses. It is usually aged in casks and is produced all around the world, and there are countless different varieties. For mixing, I favour strong, dark rums from Jamaica to produce drinks with a good body. For elegant and finessed rum beverages, I like to use younger rum varieties from Havana or Demerara.

### COGNAC

This is one of the best known types of brandy with a protected designation of origin. Aged in casks and usually a blend of various vintages, the youngest brand of Cognac V.S.O.P. (Very Superior Old Pale) must be laid down for at least four years in an oak barrel, and for XO (Extra Old), the minimum period is ten years. Instead of Cognac, you can also use Armagnac, Spanish brandy, or German brandy that has been cask aged for several years.

## TEQUILA AND MEZCAL

Both of these are made from agaves. Tequila must be produced using the blue Weber agave from the Mexican region of Jalisco or just a few other Mexican districts. This limitation makes mezcal really interesting as by contrast it can be distilled from any number of other superb agave varieties, including wild agaves. An example of a particularly special type is Mezcal de Pechuga, a smoky spirit from Mexico in which alcoholic vapours rise through raw chickens that are hung inside the still, which imparts the flavours of the chicken into the mezcal.

## SINGLE MALT WHISKY

A single malt is a whisky that stems from just one distillery. Strictly speaking malt whisky is distilled beer from malted barley, which is subsequently stored in pre-used casks. The most common are old bourbon casks, but any other kind of spirit or wine may have previously been stored in these and will influence the malt whisky accordingly. Whiskies from the Isle of Islay are characterized by their strong peaty flavour because the malted barley is dried over a peat fire. For mixing up "peat bombs" I like to use Ardbeg Ten, while for punchy drinks I love the powerful crispness of the highland whisky Nàdurra from Glenlivet. By the way, you can also try out my single malt recipes using any single malt you happen to have to hand: the result is always interesting.

## BLENDED SCOTCH WHISKY

Following a centuries old tradition, light whisky blends are produced in Scotland that taste the same year in year out, regardless of the prevailing atmospheric conditions. The base is formed by a bland-tasting, high percentage grain spirit, which is then "blended" with up to 50 flavourful single malts from various distilleries. For mixing drinks, the Scotch whiskies from Johnnie Walker work very well.

## BOURBON

Bourbon is an American whisky that is made up of at least 60 per cent corn. The remainder is made from either rye or barley. Thanks to the high proportion of corn, these whiskies are very alcoholic and rather sweet tasting. When purchasing bourbon, look out for the description "Kentucky Straight Bourbon Whiskey". I like to use Bulleit bourbon for mixing.

## RYE WHISKEY

An American whisky made from at least 60 per cent rye as well as corn and barley. Rye is far drier and more delicate than corn and this is clearly discernible in the taste. The higher the proportion of rye, the drier and more distinctive the rye whiskey is. Bulleit Rye is made with 95 per cent rye, the highest proportion of any available rye whiskey. This dry crispness is particularly well suited for classic drinks.

I often like to mix up drinks using antique glasses and utensils because this is unbelievably exciting and feels like travelling through time.

# JUICES

When using juices you should always place great emphasis on freshness and quality. There are some simple rules of thumb that will more or less guarantee you can't go wrong: freshly pressed is superior to shop-bought juice; ripe fruits are better than unripe or frozen products; organic products beat fruits cultivated conventionally; and hand-pressing gives better results than electric devices. My recipes make do without exotic juices and limit themselves to the most commonly available varieties. For simplicity's sake, I resort to purchased products from good suppliers for coconut, tomato, and cranberry juices.

### FRESHLY PRESSED
By "fresh" many bartenders really do mean pressed "à la minute", that is to say: from the fruit, into the drink. Since fresh juices oxidize and spoil rapidly this approach is of course the right one. Having said that, studies have shown that lime juice, for example, doesn't reach peak quality until 3–4 hours after pressing.

### USING PREPARED JUICES
I want to give you a clear conscience if you press your juices for your guests shortly before they arrive and store them in clean bottles to use throughout the evening. That's exactly what we do at the Golden Bar, too. At the end of the evening, however, the juices really will have gone past their best and shouldn't be used beyond this time, with the exception of grapefruit juice, which keeps for 3–4 days without any problem. If you have prepared too much juice, you can freeze it and use it again at a later date. To pep up defrosted citrus juices, take the peel from some fresh fruits (as far as possible without the white pith under the skin), warm it up in a saucepan with some water, and then squeeze out the essential oils over the juice. You can also use this method to make fresh juices even more aromatic as all citrus juices are enhanced by their essential oils.

### CITRUS JUICES
Limes, lemons, oranges, and grapefruit are best juiced using a hand press. Only use an electric juicer if you require large quantities.

### APPLE, PINEAPPLE, GINGER
You can't use a hand press to produce juices from apples, pineapples, or ginger. They are easy to make using a juicer (centrifuge), even in large quantities.

### CRANBERRY, TOMATO, COCONUT WATER
These juices, as explained earlier, are best bought from a good supplier, which is perfectly acceptable.

**18**

# SUGAR AND SYRUP

There's hardly a drink that can be made without sugar in one form or another. You can even set yourself a rule of thumb that a little dash of sugar syrup will enhance virtually any drink – just like the renowned pinch of salt when cooking. Using artificial sweeteners completely goes against my philosophy. Sugar is a flavour carrier whereas sweeteners are always accompanied by unpleasant background flavours. It is so much better to use proper sugar and to do so consciously, rather than let yourself be tempted down the path of using sugar substitutes, only to end up consuming more calories than you actually intended. The herbal sweetener, Stevia, can be an interesting sweetener for some tea blends, but you really need to be partial to the liquorice-like aftertaste. Agave syrup is better tolerated by diabetics, but still needs to be consumed in moderation. Deciding which sugar to use depends on your own taste as well as the type of drink or syrup you are going to use the sugar in.

### WHITE SUGAR

This is the most neutral tasting of all the sugars. Since it has a pure sweetness and doesn't distort the result with any ancillary flavours, it is perfect for producing simple sugar syrup and other recipes that require sugar. White sugar consists of sucrose, which is refined from sugar beet or sugar cane. The resulting juice is boiled and centrifuged to produce crystalline raw sugar, which must then be bleached, usually using chemicals.

### BROWN SUGAR

This is just as laborious to produce as white sugar and is then coloured using molasses.

### MUSCOVADO SUGAR

During normal sugar production the crystals are separated with the help of a centrifuge; when making muscovado sugar on the other hand, the boiled sugar cane juice is dried until it crystallizes. By pre-treating it in different ways, you get light or dark sugar. The dark variety has a very strong flavour of molasses, while the appeal of the lighter variant lies in its delicate treacle notes, which is why I love to use the latter in some of my recipes. Above all, light muscovado sugar gives syrups a lovely depth. In addition it has the highest proportion of vitamins and minerals of all the sugar varieties.

### UNREFINED SUGAR/DEMERARA SUGAR

Unrefined sugar is manufactured in the same way as white sugar, but isn't refined at the end. That means it isn't white and it naturally possesses a proportion of molasses, which give it a stronger and more full-bodied flavour. Demerara sugar is a typical unrefined sugar. I recommend using it in drinks and syrups where you want a bit more depth and breadth.

## ORGANIC SUGAR

This is primarily distinguished by the fact that the refined sugar is not allowed to be bleached chemically at the end of processing. From a flavour perspective, due to the residual proportion of molasses, it lies somewhere between unrefined sugar and white sugar.

## MOLASSES

These are the blackish-brown sugar cane juices that result from processing the sugar cane. They are often used in baking in the UK and are the raw material for all rums made from fresh sugar cane juice, except for the cane juice rums (Rhum agricole). You will need to use molasses very cautiously when mixing drinks as they have an extremely intense and distinctive flavour.

## HONEY

This is a natural sweetener that imparts a huge variety of flavours and sweetness depending on the type of flower and its origin. It is essential for recipes where its distinctive full flavour plays a major role. Runny honey is discussed on page 160. A little spritz of this rounds off many drinks.

## AGAVE SYRUP/AGAVE JUICE CONCENTRATE

This liquid form of sugar works particularly well in drinks with mezcal or tequila because they are produced from the same raw material: the agave. Agave syrup became known among bartenders through Julio Bermejo from Tommy's Bar in Los Angeles who used it in Tommy's Margarita. The aroma is sometimes slightly grassy, the sweetness is stronger than in normal sugar syrup thanks to the higher proportion of fructose, and the syrup is less viscose on the tongue.

## SYRUPS

In the Basic Recipes chapter (see pp.158–162) you will find recipes for all the syrups used in the book, from the simple sugar syrup (simple syrup) to highly aromatic varieties based on fruits, tea, or malt beer. Making your own syrups might be somewhat more time-consuming, but it is fun and gives you an opportunity to create flavours that can't be bought in any shop, especially if you use modern preparation techniques such as sous vide, pressure infusion, or the freezer method, all of which I describe in the Appendix. Making a syrup really is worth the effort, not least because the quality, even on your first attempts, will be far better than in any purchased product, although of course you can always use these, too.

## MY TIP

Play around with a recipe using different sources of sugar to experience the important role played by each.

# ICE

Ice is one of the most important factors for a good drink. When I talk about solid ice in my recipes, I mean large, clear, full ice cubes with edges around 3cm (1in) long. Little cones with a hole, nuggets, or shards are a no-no. And make sure that everything is prepared with the utmost cleanliness at each stage of the process!

### ICE CUBES

To make these professionally, you ideally need filtered water and rectangular silicon moulds from a good kitchen stockist. Fill the moulds, then place in a tray filled with water, so that the water just covers the moulds, and freeze. Once frozen carefully free the ice moulds from the frozen block, chipping away the excess ice from the edges. Remove the ice cubes from the silicon moulds. This produces double-frozen ice, which is used in many of the top bars. This method is ideal for ice added to stirred drinks, which should be kept extremely cold and require very little "melt" water. For domestic use, bags of ice are also widely available. Or you can ask a nearby bar, who may be happy to top up your supplies now and then in exchange for an appropriate tip. Anyone who wishes to acquire an ice-making machine for a professional bar should consider getting one size bigger than they estimate they need to ensure they will have sufficient ice.

### CRUSHED ICE

The best crushed ice is made by taking double frozen ice cubes and crushing them in an ice crusher or Thermomix before subsequently freezing them again, stirring them up repeatedly while they are freezing. The result is a fine granularity with optimum cooling characteristics. Alternatively, you can crush the ice cubes in a clean linen bag using a wooden hammer or similar.

### ICE BLOCKS AND ICE CHUNKS

For self-hewn ice you need a clear block of ice, which you can order from an ice supplier, or the internet. I have a preference for using large chunks of ice that have been chipped off an ice block. If you want to make your own clear block of ice, fill a Thermobox of the required size with distilled or filtered water and place this without a lid in the freezer. The ice block will freeze through from top to bottom until it is crystal clear, apart from a dull strip on the base, which you will need to chip off using an ice saw or ice pick.

### ICE BALLS

Ice balls are usually carved by hand, but to make these at home I use water bomb balloons. Fill the balloons with filtered water, tie them, and place them in the freezer so that they lie more or less spherically. This method results in slightly cloudy balls, but the advantage is you have hygienic individual packaging which is easy to handle.

# PREPARATION:
# SHAKEN, STIRRED...

With the appropriate equipment and a couple of simple steps you can mix up practically any drink. Only the shaker requires a bit of practice. The photos on the following pages show you how to handle the most important tools and ingredients.

### 1 SHAKEN

Place the ingredients in the shaker with ice for a wet shake, or without ice for a dry shake, close the lid, and shake vigorously for 10–15 seconds. By shaking with ice the drink not only gets chilled, but also some melt water is transferred into the drink – how much of this you want depends on the type of drink. After around 90 seconds, the drink won't get any colder and it will hardly absorb any more melt water. To practice, you can half fill the shaker with uncooked grains of rice, which has a similar feel to shaking with drink ingredients and ice.

### 2 STIRRED

As a rule, all the ingredients for a drink are stirred together for 10–15 seconds in a mixing glass. While stirring for longer will make the drink colder, it also dilutes it more; something which is actually desirable in certain drinks. After around 90 seconds, just as with shaking, the drink won't change much more.

### 3 BUILT IN THE GLASS

This is how we describe mixing together and stirring all the ingredients on ice in the customer's glass. Cocktails such as the Old Fashioned, Rasta Nail, and all long drinks, such as the Moscow Mule, for example, are built up in the glass.

### 4 PREPARED IN THE BOTTLE

All drinks with this symbol • • • can be prepared and kept cool until your guests arrive. These drinks are therefore ideal for larger gatherings or parties. Preparing something ahead in the bottle is nothing to be ashamed of: as far back as 150 years ago, professional bartenders were using this technique to help cope with sudden peaks in demand. Not only do you save time this way, but also every drink is of the same quality because the recipe is accurately measured out only once. Simply take the specified quantity of ingredients for the recipe and multiply by the number of guests, mix it all up in a larger container, decant into clean bottles, and store in the fridge. Before use, shake briefly and carry out any additional steps according to the recipe. To compensate for the lack of melt water, you should add a splash of water to clear bottled drinks.

24

# ...STRAINED

Whether you use a Hawthorne or a julep strainer, the main concern is that only the ingredients that ultimately belong in the drink actually end up in the glass. The origin of the julep strainer dates back to when people would have used a strainer while drinking a classic julep cocktail, placing it on the cup to avoid swallowing little bits of ice or mint.

### 5 STRAINING OR FILTERING

This has to be done for almost all drinks that are prepared in a shaker or mixing glass. Hold the strainer at the opening of the shaker or mixing glass and pour the drink through the sieve into the drinking glass.

### 6 DOUBLE STRAINING OR FINE FILTERING

These are the terms used for straining drinks to filter out any tiny pieces of ice, fruit, or herbs that don't belong in the drinking glass. To do this, a little tea strainer is held between the strainer and the glass.

### 7 & 8 SQUEEZING CITRUS ZEST

Thinly slice a piece of peel from your citrus fruit and squeeze it over the drink. Citrus zest will imbue the drink with a wonderful aroma, but the remaining peel shouldn't be added to the drink because it contains a lot of bitter substances that will flavour the drink too strongly. Exceptions to this rule are recipes where precisely this effect is desired. In these cases, care should be taken that the zest is free of any white pith because this is particularly bitter.

### SQUEEZE (NO PICTURE)

If a squeeze is required, take a little slice of citrus fruit, for example, one-sixth of a lime, squeeze this over the drink, and then add the slice to the drink.

### CRUSTA (NO PICTURE)

To create a "crusta" (sugared rim), moisten the edge of the glass and dip it into a plate covered with sugar – how deep and for how long depends on the desired width and hardness of the crusta. Countless varieties of crusta can be made using different sugars and liquids. A particularly fine crusta can be made by spraying the top of the glass with the appropriate liqueur from an atomizer and then turning it in sugar or powder to coat.

THE RECIPES

# SIMPLE

AND

# CLEVER

EASY-TO-MIX DRINKS

FOR

FOR EVERY OCCASION

# GOLDEN CHAMPAGNE

The Golden Champagne is one of our house aperitifs at the Golden Bar. Just as fine in summer as in winter, this is the ideal starter. What's more, it is brilliantly suited for larger parties because you can prepare the base in advance, decant it into bottles, and keep it cold until you are ready to use it. You can even perfume the glasses in advance. Just don't pour out the champagne until your guests arrive. This ensures the perlage, or "beads", on the champagne isn't lost and, it's a nice gesture to prepare the drink in front of your guests before handing them the freshly sparkling cocktail.

**INGREDIENTS**
FRESH SAGE
30 ML (1 FL OZ) TANQUERAY NO.
  TEN GIN
1 TBSP FRESH LEMON JUICE
2 TSP ELDERFLOWER SYRUP
  (SEE P.159)
2 DASHES ORANGE BITTERS
PERRIER JOUËT GRAND BRUT
  CHAMPAGNE

**CHAMPAGNE FLUTE OR
SILVER GOBLET**

**PREPARATION**
Fold a sage leaf between thumb and index finger and rub the edge of the glass with the leaf to perfume it. Vigorously shake gin, lemon, syrup, and bitters in a shaker with solid ice and double strain into the glass. Carefully top up with champagne. Add a pretty sage leaf to the drink as decoration.

**Elderflower and sage are perfect partners in combination with gin.**

30

# WILLIAMS SOUR

Mixing drinks using top-quality fruit brandies is incredibly good fun. Simple classics work best here because the spirit always plays a leading role in these kinds of drinks. In my opinion, the best quality brandies are the Austrian Reisetbauer varieties.

**INGREDIENTS**
½ EGG WHITE
50ML (1¾FL OZ) WILLIAMS PEAR
  BRANDY
1 TBSP FRESH LEMON JUICE
1 TBSP FRESH LIME JUICE
2 BSP ICING SUGAR

SMALL COCKTAIL GLASS

**PREPARATION**
Divide the egg white by allowing half to run into the shaker and then halt the flow using a knife with a wide blade. Shake up all the ingredients in the shaker with solid ice and then double strain into a small pre-chilled cocktail glass (see picture, right).

# PLUM FIZZ

As with the Williams Sour, I use lime and lemon juice in equal proportions here. This lends the drink a finer acidity structure.

**INGREDIENTS**
50ML (1¾FL OZ) PLUM BRANDY
1 TBSP FRESH LEMON JUICE
1 TBSP FRESH LIME JUICE
2 BSP ICING SUGAR
1 EGG WHITE
SODA

HIGHBALL

**PREPARATION**
Vigorously shake all the ingredients except the soda in a shaker with solid ice and strain into a pre-chilled highball glass. Top up with a generous shot of soda and serve immediately. The drink tastes best when ice cold and freshly sparkling (see picture, left).

# KYOTO ROSE FIZZ

This is one of my favourite recipes using sake. The silky structure that the egg white gives to the drink goes beguilingly well with the delicate aromas of the orange blossom water and the dried rose petals, which can be found in herbal remedy shops and many supermarkets. In the original recipe, which I created in 2012 as one of the 7 Samurai head bartenders, I use rosé sake. Since good-quality sources of this are rather trickier to find, I have reconstructed the flavour profile using normal sake along with Lillet rosé. If you ever happen to come across a really decent rosé sake – you absolutely must try it!

## INGREDIENTS
50ML (1¾FL OZ) JUNMAI GINJO
   SAKE
20ML (¾FL OZ) LILLET ROSÉ
1 TBSP FRESH LIME JUICE
1 TBSP FRESH LEMON JUICE
1 DASH SUGAR SYRUP
   (SEE P.158)
2 BSP ICING SUGAR
2 DASHES ORANGE BLOSSOM
   WATER
1 EGG WHITE
DRIED ROSE PETALS
SODA

**LONG DRINK GLASS**

## PREPARATION
Vigorously shake all the ingredients except for the soda in a shaker with solid ice for 10–15 seconds and then strain into a long drink glass filled with ice. Mix with a touch of soda water.

You can also add the little shot of soda directly to the shaker after mixing. This will make the drink more homogeneous.

# GINTELLIGENCE NO. 1

The template for this hot drink is the classic Tom Collins, which is often confused with the Fizz. In composition these two are almost identical; however, the Fizz is served in a pre-chilled glass without ice and mixed with a shot of soda, while the Collins is served in a long drink glass and diluted with lots of soda. Gintelligence No. 1 got its name because I discovered quite accidentally how fantastic this renowned concoction tasted warm: a crafty drink to warm you up on cold days in autumn and winter. It has an even fuller, stronger flavour if you use Dutch style gin (Jenever) instead.

**INGREDIENTS**
60ML (2FL OZ) TANQUERAY NO.
  TEN OR DUTCH STYLE GIN
30ML (1FL OZ) FRESH LEMON
  JUICE
20ML (¾FL OZ) TRIPLE SYRUP
  (SEE P.160)
5 JUNIPER BERRIES
100ML (3½FL OZ) HOT WATER

**TEA CUP OR MISO SOUP BOWL**

**PREPARATION**
Heat all the ingredients except for the water in a saucepan or silver pot on the stove and top up with hot water. Place the juniper berries in the tea cup and serve the drink in the cup or soup bowl.

Silver has a particularly
high thermal conductivity
and keeps drinks warm, or
indeed cold, for longer.

# MR SERIOUS CHAMPAGNE COCKTAIL

I am one of those people who sometimes prefer to observe rather than do the talking. Thanks to this preference I earned myself the nickname Mr Serious at Appleton in Jamaica, one of the largest rum distilleries in the Caribbean. This inspired me to invent a drink that doesn't require you to talk much and which you can just enjoy quietly. For this recipe (as with most of my drinks) you can replace the Sexy Bitters with Angostura bitters. Alternatively, try out the aromatic bitters following the recipe on page 156.

**INGREDIENTS**
20ML (¾FL OZ) DARK JAMAICAN
  RUM
2 TSP FALERNUM (SEE P.159)
1 SQUEEZE OF FRESH LIME
2 DASHES SEXY BITTERS
PERRIER JOUËT GRAND BRUT
  CHAMPAGNE

**CHAMPAGNE FLUTE OR
SILVER GOBLET**

**PREPARATION**
Vigorously shake all the ingredients except the champagne in a shaker with solid ice and strain into a pre-chilled champagne flute or silver goblet. Top up with ice-cold dry champagne.

Pre-chill glasses
in the fridge. Or
add crushed ice to the
glass, then tip this
away before you pour
in the drink.

# SAMURAI SPIRIT

Sake and cranberries are a fantastic combination, particularly if enjoyed warm. However, you need to pay attention to the following: never heat good-quality sake for drinking neat higher than 40–50°C (104–122°F). Only poorer qualities are heated any higher because this helps to mask deficiencies in taste and quality. The same applies to mixed drinks with sake, although you can go a little higher with the temperature here.

**INGREDIENTS**

20ML (¾FL OZ) RUNNY HONEY
  (SEE P.160)
5 THIN SLICES (2MM) FRESH
  UNPEELED GINGER
100ML (3½FL OZ) JUNMAI GINJO
  SAKE
2 DASHES LEMON BITTERS
50ML (1¾FL OZ) CRANBERRY
  JUICE
2 CARDAMOM PODS

SMALL SAUCEPAN OR
SILVER POT

SMALL CUP

**PREPARATION**

Place the honey and ginger in the pan or pot and press them with a muddler to mingle the flavours. Add the sake, lemon bitters, and cranberry juice and heat gently on the hob, or with the steam nozzle of an espresso machine, to 50–60°C (122–140°F). The best way to control the temperature is with a roasting thermometer. Press down on the cardamom pods, place them in the cup, and strain the drink into the cup.

For warm sake drinks always use dry (karakuchi) sake. This becomes sweeter as you heat it and you save on sugar.

# HOME-MADE GINGER BEER

Yes, yes, yes, the whole thing with ginger beer versus ginger ale is all rather confusing. In the 18th century, ginger beer wasn't made using carbon dioxide, but relied instead on yeast, which resulted in the production of a certain amount of alcohol. For this reason, it became a victim of the American prohibition. An artificially flavoured carbonated ginger drink was created as an alcohol-free alternative, and this is still known today as ginger ale. This has become an indispensable ingredient in certain drinks, but for my own recipes I use only ginger beer, which is completely different in character from ginger ale. While you can easily buy ginger beer nowadays, nothing can rival the taste of home-made versions. And my method is so simple... you really must try it out!

**INGREDIENTS**
1 PART FRESH GINGER JUICE
1.5–2 PARTS SUGAR SYRUP
  (SEE P.158)
3 PARTS FRESH LEMON JUICE
10 PARTS TAP WATER OR STILL
  MINERAL WATER

**PREPARATION**
Pour the juices through a fine sieve and mix with the other ingredients. Pour a litre of this into a soda syphon and feed in a $CO_2$ capsule. Ideally, chill for 3 hours so that the carbon dioxide bonds better with the liquid – and you're done. For those of you who love a bit of experimentation, rather than carbonating the mixture in a syphon, do this in a bottle with the addition of champagne yeast (24 yeast cubes/24 hours fermentation) and await the result with eager anticipation.

For a quick version without a soda syphon, use highly carbonated mineral water instead of still water.

# MOSCOW MULE & CO.

Here are a few suggestions for using the delicious home-made ginger beer (see p.42). In the Golden Bar, we serve ginger beer hot or cold and without any extras all day long: just a generous squeeze of orange into the glass or cup and enjoy. When enjoyed cold this is a deliciously refreshing beverage, and when heated it is a tasty, warming medicinal substance that you can drink cup after cup of without a care, even if you haven't got a cold. My personal favourite is the non-alcoholic "sexy" ginger beer – with a couple of dashes of Sexy Bitters and a large squeeze of orange. A Moscow Mule is traditionally served in a copper mug.

**INGREDIENTS FOR ALL VARIANTS**
50ML (1¾FL OZ) SPIRIT
120ML (4FL OZ) HOME-MADE
  GINGER BEER
DECORATION

**LONG DRINK GLASS**

A spirit plus ginger beer is called a "Mule". If you add a squeeze of lime, it's called a "buck".

FOR AN ALCOHOLIC VARIETY JUST CHOOSE YOUR FAVOURITE SPIRIT, OR TRY ONE OF THE FOLLOWING CLASSICS:

**MOSCOW MULE** –
with vodka, garnished with a slice of cucumber

**ISLAY MULE** –
with Ardbeg Ten or another smoky single malt

**LONDON BUCK** –
with gin, garnished with a squeeze of fresh lime

**DARK & STORMY** –
with Goslings Black Seal rum and a little squeeze of fresh lime

**SHOCHU BUDO SHOGA** –
with shochu and a shot of red grape juice

**PREPARATION**
Build up all the ingredients on ice in the glass.

# SANTINO

The Crodino that I use for this drink is an Italian carbonated non-alcoholic bitter aperitif. Similar to Sanbitter, its lovely bitter-fruity notes lend complexity and depth to produce wonderful non-alcoholic beverages.

## INGREDIENTS
100ML (3½FL OZ) CRODINO
20ML (¾FL OZ) FRESH
    PINEAPPLE JUICE
100ML (3½FL OZ) GINGER BEER
    (SEE P.42)
5 THIN (2MM/¼IN) SLICES
    CUCUMBER

**LARGE WINE GLASS**

## PREPARATION
Fill the wine glass to the brim with ice and pour a little bottle of Crodino over the ice. Add the pineapple juice and top up with the ginger beer. Stick slices of cucumber into the drink and stir gently.

Cucumber and
pineapple are aromatically
perfect partners.

# BANKSY

In the Golden Bar we are open to all suggestions. But even so we feel that the era of heavy, cream-laden cocktails is long since over. If we want to gently persuade a customer who is really after a piña colada to opt for an equally sinful alternative, it's usually enough just to list the indulgent ingredients of our Banksy: fine white rum, fresh pineapple juice, organic coconut water. That's all it takes to enthuse most people. I've dedicated this drink to my favourite graffiti artist Banksy – perhaps you've already noticed the little play on words with the top class rum that is used in this drink.

**INGREDIENTS**
60ML (2FL OZ) WHITE RUM,
   SUCH AS BANKS 5 ISLAND
40ML (1¼FL OZ) FRESH
   PINEAPPLE JUICE
40ML (1¼FL OZ) ORGANIC
   COCONUT WATER
A FEW DASHES OF SUGAR
   SYRUP (SEE P.158), ACCORDING
   TO TASTE

**COCKTAIL GLASS**

**PREPARATION**
Place all the ingredients in a shaker with solid ice and shake vigorously. Depending on the sweetness of the pineapple juice, if necessary round things off with a couple of additional splashes of sugar syrup. Double strain into a pre-chilled cocktail glass.

To add amazing roasted notes to the drink, before juicing caramelize the pineapple pieces in a pan until they are golden brown.

# BISHOP

Some drinks don't just taste great, but also work simultaneously as a medicinal home remedy. Ginger, honey, vitamins, and the tried and tested herbal concoction Chartreuse (see p.165) all help you get back on your feet when you've got a cold.

**INGREDIENTS**
5 THIN SLICES (2MM/¼IN)
 UNPEELED FRESH GINGER
1 BSP HONEY
80ML (2¾FL OZ) HOT WATER
20–40ML (¾–1¼FL OZ) GREEN
 CHARTREUSE V. E. P.

**SMALL CUP**

**PREPARATION**
Press the honey and ginger together in the cup so that the flavours and juice of the ginger combine with the sweetness of the honey. Top up with hot, but not boiling, water. Add green Chartreuse V.E.P according to taste and drink hot (see picture, left).

# RESCUE REMEDY PUNCH

Enjoyed shortly before going to sleep, this drink really will make you sweat overnight, which can do you good if you have a cold, and often helps relieve cold symptoms.

**INGREDIENTS**
40ML (1¼FL OZ) ABSINTHE
 DUPLAIS VERTE
80ML (2¾FL OZ) GINGER BEER
 (SEE P.42)

**SMALL TEA CUP OR**
**HEAT-RESISTANT GLASS**

**PREPARATION**
Gently heat both ingredients in a small pan, or with the steam nozzle of an espresso machine, but do not boil. Serve in a little tea cup or a heat-resistant glass (see picture, right).

# EAST VILLAGE

A couple of years ago – when I was working with my esteemed colleague Stefan Gabayi at Schumann's in Munich – we were inspired by H. I. Williams' classic *3 Bottle Bar* from 1943 and we set out to make some drinks following the premise of his book: that all recipes should be made using just three different spirits. This is the origin of the East Village, which has developed over time to become one of our bestselling modern classics. In the original recipe the sake was backed up with a little shot of gin, but nowadays I prefer the lighter version without any gin.

## INGREDIENTS

60ML (2FL OZ) JUNMAI GINJO
  SAKE
1 BSP RASPBERRY SYRUP
  (SEE P.159)
1 TSP ORANGE CURAÇAO
30ML (1FL OZ) CRANBERRY
  JUICE
1 SMALL SQUEEZE OF LIME
1 PIECE ORANGE ZEST FOR
  SQUEEZING

COCKTAIL GLASS

## PREPARATION

Vigorously shake all the ingredients with solid ice and strain into a pre-chilled cocktail glass. Add the scent of a little orange zest.

Sake goes really well
with red fruits such
as cranberries or
raspberries.

# GOLDEN BRAMBLE

It doesn't take much to give simple drinks a certain little something extra. Here a small injection gives a great "Aha!" effect, which is even greater with the grilled lemon juice described below.

**INGREDIENTS**
50ML (1¾FL OZ) TANQUERAY NO. TEN GIN
30ML (1FL OZ) FRESH LEMON JUICE
2 BSP ICING SUGAR
20ML (¾FL OZ) ORANGE LIQUEUR SUCH AS BIGALLET CHINA CHINA OR AMER PICON

SMALL CANNULA
COCKTAIL GLASS

**PREPARATION**
Vigorously shake the gin, juice, and sugar in a shaker with solid ice and strain into a glass filled with crushed ice. Top up with some more crushed ice. Put the orange liqueur into the cannula and stick cannula into the drink. Inject the orange liqueur into the drink just before drinking (see picture, right).

# HIBISCO DE JALISCO

To make "grilled" citrus juice, place the halved lemon or lime with its cut surface face down in a hot pan without any oil until it is appetizingly bronzed, then juice it. This gives a wonderful roasted flavour.

**INGREDIENTS**
1 LIME
HIBISCUS SUGAR (SEE P.162)
50ML (1¾FL OZ) WHITE TEQUILA
30ML (1FL OZ) FRESH LIME JUICE
1 TBSP TRIPLE SYRUP (SEE P.160)
2 TSP CHAMBORD BERRY LIQUEUR

COCKTAIL GLASS

**PREPARATION**
Moisten the outer rim of the cocktail glass with the cut surface of the lime and dip the rim in the hibiscus sugar so that it acquires a roughly 1cm (½in) wide crust. Vigorously shake together the tequila, lime juice, and triple syrup with solid ice in a shaker and double strain it into the glass. Pour the Chambord into the centre of the drink, and allow to settle on the base of the glass (see picture, left).

# TOXIC GARDEN

If you ever needed proof that non-alcoholic drinks don't have to turn out dull, overly sweet, and unsubtle, here it is. Instead of mint you could also substitute other fresh herbs or choose a combination. Just take a little trip out to your kitchen garden: thyme, basil, Thai basil, nettles, or even salad leaves – anything is possible. By the way, up until the middle of the 1950s the lemonade 7 Up was sold exclusively in pharmacies and was considered a gentle medication for combatting depression. Although it no longer contains pharmaceutical substances, the recipe is still crisp, fresh, and unmistakable.

**INGREDIENTS**

A SMALL HANDFUL OF FRESH
  MINT LEAVES OR OTHER HERBS
3 DASHES CELERY BITTERS
2 TSP ELDERFLOWER SYRUP
  (SEE P.159)
100ML (3½FL OZ) LEMONADE
  SUCH AS 7 UP
100ML (3½FL OZ) EXTRA DRY
  TONIC WATER
3–4 THIN (2MM/¼IN) SLICES OF
  CUCUMBER

**LONG DRINK GLASS**

**PREPARATION**

Place the mint leaves or other herbs with some ice in a long drink glass and pour over the bitters, elderflower syrup, lemonade, and tonic water. Add the cucumber slices to the drink. Stir gently once again and serve.

# KLAUS OF PAIN

Tiki Time! This drink is pretty strong and guarantees success at every party since it aids endurance with a touch of caffeine, vitamin C, and fresh ginger. You can mix it up with home-made ingredients or fall back on one of the less exciting variants made completely with shop-bought products. Both will work, but, just as with all the other drinks, it's really worth investing the extra effort involved in the home-made version. Take your time. Your guests will thank you for it.

**INGREDIENTS**
60ML (2FL OZ) DARK JAMAICAN
  RUM
2 TSP WRAY & NEPHEW WHITE
  OVERPROOF RUM
2 TSP AGAVE COFFEE (SEE P.163)
  OR TIA MARIA
40ML (1¼FL OZ) FRESH
  PINEAPPLE JUICE
6 DASHES SEXY BITTERS
40ML (1¼FL OZ) GINGER BEER
  (SEE P.42)

**TIKI MUG**
**OR LARGE LONG DRINK GLASS**
**(AROUND 300ML/10FL OZ)**

**PREPARATION**
Shake all the ingredients except for the ginger beer in a shaker with solid ice and strain into a tiki mug or large glass that has been filled with crushed ice. Top up with ginger beer and fresh crushed ice. Add some fancy decorations and serve.

One of the few tiki drinks without citric acid (except in the ginger beer). Highly recommended for those with sensitive stomachs!

# YAMAHAI

Gin and sake complement each other perfectly. In this twist on an improved gin cocktail the fruity notes of Tanqueray No. Ten combine beautifully with the gentle floral notes of the first rate Daiginjo sake.

**INGREDIENTS**
1 UNREFINED SUGAR CUBE
30ML (1FL OZ) TANQUERAY NO. TEN GIN
30ML (1FL OZ) JUNMAI DAIGINJO SAKE
2 DASHES ORANGE BITTERS
1 PIECE LEMON ZEST FOR SQUEEZING

OLD FASHIONED GLASS

**PREPARATION**
Place all the ingredients in the glass. Crush the sugar cubes with the end of a spoon and stir until they dissolve. Then add ice cubes and stir until sufficient meltwater has been produced that the glass is full to about a finger width below the rim. Squeeze a little bit of lemon zest over the drink (see picture, right).

# ICHIGO ICHIE

In Japan, Ichigo Ichie stands for a chance meeting, the perfect first impression – as perfect as the union of Junmai sake with gin and vermouth.

**INGREDIENTS**
20ML (¾FL OZ) TANQUERAY NO. TEN GIN
40ML (1¼FL OZ) JUNMAI SAKE
40ML (1¼FL OZ) CARPANO ANTICA FORMULA VERMOUTH
ORANGE AND LEMON ZEST FOR SQUEEZING

SMALL BEAKER

**PREPARATION**
Stir all the ingredients in the beaker with lots of ice, and squeeze over a little bit of orange and lemon zest (see picture, left).

# LEMMY KILMISTER'S RUM GROG

Of course, this wasn't Lemmy's favourite drink, because every kid knows that the lead singer of Motörhead preferred to drink Jack Daniel's with Coke when he was at the pinball machine. So why have I dedicated one of my favourite hot drinks to the greatest rock star of all time? Because it barely takes more time to create than a guitar solo which, according to Lemmy, should never take longer than the time needed to open a bottle of beer.

## INGREDIENTS
60ML (2FL OZ) STRONG DARK
　RUM
2 BSP FIG JAM
1 TBSP FALERNUM (SEE P.159)
20ML (¾FL OZ) FRESH LEMON
　JUICE
40ML (1¼FL OZ) FRESH ORANGE
　JUICE
40ML (1¼FL OZ) HOT WATER
2 PIECES OF STAR ANISE
FRESH ROSEMARY

**LARGE CUP OR HEAT-
RESISTANT GLASS WITH
A HANDLE**

## PREPARATION
Heat all the ingredients except the star anise and rosemary in a small pan and pour into a pre-warmed cup or glass. Top up with a generous shot of hot water and decorate with the sprig of rosemary and star anise. Finally, if you like, set the rosemary needles alight to really bring out the smoke and aroma.

**Have the Motörhead album
*Bastards* playing while you
prepare this!**

# FRESH PALOMA

The Paloma, the national drink of Mexico, has also made a big breakthrough in northern latitudes over recent years. It's an exquisite refreshment, especially in summer, albeit somewhat lethal. The salt gives the drink a particular kick and provides the body with electrolytes, which can help combat a hangover. Here again it is really worth the effort to make the lemonade yourself because it's pretty simple and it tastes even better. For a delicious non-alcoholic version, leave out the tequila and just put a bouquet of fresh mint in the drink.

**INGREDIENTS**
50ML (1¾FL OZ) WHITE TEQUILA
ONE PINCH SEA SALT, SUCH AS
  FLEUR DE SEL
1–2 SQUEEZES FRESH LIME
120ML (4FL OZ) PINK GRAPEFRUIT
  LEMONADE (SEE BELOW)

**LONG DRINK GLASS**

**PREPARATION**
Stir the tequila, sea salt, and lime with ice in a long drink glass and top up with pink grapefruit lemonade.

**PINK GRAPEFRUIT LEMONADE**

**INGREDIENTS**
1 PART FRESH LEMON JUICE
1 PART SUGAR SYRUP (SEE P.158)
6 PARTS FRESH PINK
  GRAPEFRUIT JUICE
6 PARTS TAP WATER OR STILL
  MINERAL WATER

**PREPARATION**
Finely strain the juices after squeezing so that the fruit pulp doesn't clog up the syphon. Mix together all the ingredients, put a litre into a soda syphon, and fill with 1–2 $CO_2$ capsules. Ideally leave to chill for 3 hours before use so that the carbon dioxide bonds better with the liquid. If you don't own a soda syphon you can use highly carbonated mineral water instead of the still water.

# WALTHER PPK

I have a close friendship with Mirko Hecktor, the ballet dancer, artist, DJ, and producer. This drink is dedicated to him and named after the Walther PPK club, an event concept on the Munich club scene, which is where we got to know each other many years ago. The drink is pretty strong and contains everything we like to start off a long night.

**INGREDIENTS**
1 SPRAY ABSINTHE, SUCH AS
 DUPLAIS VERTE
40ML (1¼FL OZ) CHOCOLATE
 SPIRIT OR CHOCOLATE LIQUOR,
 SUCH AS MOZART DRY
20ML (¾FL OZ) MINT LIQUEUR
 SUCH AS BRANCA MENTA
1 DASH ANGOSTURA BITTERS

**COCKTAIL GLASS**

Pour the absinthe into a little atomizer and use it to moisten the inside of the glass. This helps the aroma of the absinthe to integrate quite subtly into the drink. Shake all the other ingredients with solid ice in the shaker and double strain into the cocktail glass.

A little glass of absinthe
at the start of a long night
helps the liver process
alcohol better.

# ARSHAVIN

As in many of my mainly non-alcoholic recipes, I use slightly alcoholic cocktail bitters here. The taste is important to give the drink greater depth. All in all this contains a lower percentage of alcohol than a low-alcohol beer.

**INGREDIENTS**
100ML (3½FL OZ) RHUBARB
 JUICE
100ML (3½FL OZ) GINGER BEER
 (SEE P.42)
5 DASHES PEYCHAUD'S BITTERS
2 SQUEEZES PINK GRAPEFRUIT

**LARGE WINE GLASS**

**PREPARATION**
Fill the wine glass with large ice cubes. Add the juice, ginger beer, and bitters and stir gently. Squeeze in two large segments of grapefruit before adding the segments to the drink (see picture, right).

# BITTERMAN'S FRIEND

And here's another virtually alcohol-free suggestion for fans of bitter fruit flavours and complexity. After this drink you can get behind the steering wheel with a clear conscience.

**INGREDIENTS**
100ML (3½FL OZ) SANBITTER
100ML (3½FL OZ) GINGER BEER
 (SEE P.42)
5 DASHES PEYCHAUD'S BITTERS
2 SQUEEZES ORANGE

**LARGE WINE GLASS**

**PREPARATION**
Fill the wine glass with large ice cubes, pour the ingredients over, and stir briefly. Gently squeeze over two large orange segments and add them to the drink (see picture, left).

# MUNICH ICED COFFEE

Munich iced coffee was already well established by the 1950s and in those days was served using filter coffee on ice with whipped cream. This still works wonderfully well, of course, but I far prefer the version made with coffee concentrate, or a cold drip coffee, and a touch of just very lightly whipped cream. The coffee concentrate has the advantage of keeping for up to two weeks in the fridge without losing any flavour. Cold drip coffee doesn't keep as long, but the coffee is highly aromatic and its fruity notes are particularly refreshing on hot days.

**INGREDIENTS**
120ML (4FL OZ) COFFEE
  CONCENTRATE OR COLD DRIP
  (SEE BELOW)
CREAM, LIGHTLY WHIPPED

**HIGHBALL OR SMALL BEAKER**

**PREPARATION**
Pour coffee concentrate into a highball glass that has been filled with large ice cubes and top with cream that has been whipped until it is just holding its shape.

## COFFEE CONCENTRATE

You can also make the following recipe in a French press cafetière by adjusting the quantities in accordance with the volume of your container. For a cold dripper (see p.12) use 80g (3oz) freshly ground coffee to 1 litre (1¾ pints) water. You should choose a 100 per cent arabica fairtrade coffee.

**INGREDIENTS**
240G (8½OZ) COFFEE,
  COARSELY GROUND
1 LITRE (1¾ PINTS) COLD
  WATER

**PREPARATION**
Mix the coffee and water and leave to steep for 8–12 hours. Then filter and dilute with water before use in a ratio of 1:3.

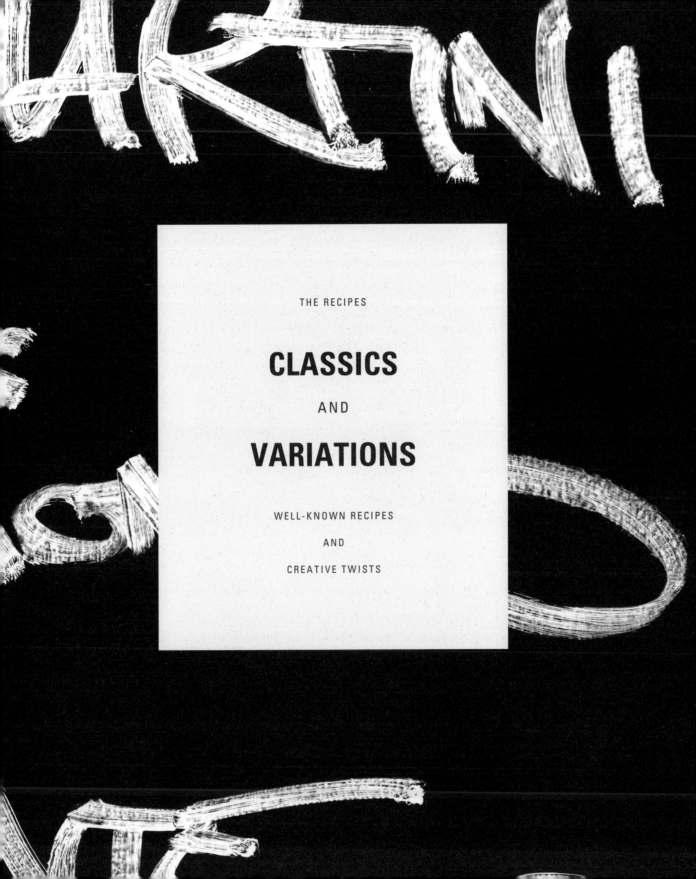

THE RECIPES

# CLASSICS

AND

# VARIATIONS

WELL-KNOWN RECIPES

AND

CREATIVE TWISTS

# COLD DUCK 2011

Over a hundred years ago the Cold Duck was already a popular refreshing beverage made from champagne, white wine, and carbonated water mixed with lemon zest. In my version from 2011 I forgo the wine and round off the flavours of this sparkling spritzer with some camomile syrup. For a party just multiply the ingredients by the number of guests and then double or triple the quantities again according to thirst. The fresh blossoms look lovely in a large punch bowl. They are not only aesthetically pleasing, but also lend a delicate floral aroma to the mix.

**INGREDIENTS**
1 ORGANIC LEMON
100ML (3½FL OZ) PERRIER JOUËT
  GRAND BRUT CHAMPAGNE
100ML (3½FL OZ) SODA
2 TSP CAMOMILE SYRUP
  (SEE P.159)
EDIBLE PETALS, FRESH OR DRIED

LARGE WINE GLASS

**PREPARATION**
Slice off the ends of the lemon and peel the fruit carefully all around, as with an apple, to create a long strip of zest. Fill the glass with ice cubes and drape the lemon zest in a spiral shape inside the glass. Carefully pour in the champagne and top up with the soda. Pour over the camomile syrup and decorate with petals.

In Vienna the champagne spritzer is known as a "fine spritzer".

# DRY MARTINI

One of the earliest mentions of the Martini cocktail is found in Thomas Stuart's book *Stuart's Fancy Drinks and How to Mix Them* from 1896: a well-balanced beverage consisting of one-third dry French vermouth, two-thirds dry gin, bitters, and the zest of a lemon. Unfortunately over the last century the Dry Martini has degenerated into a simple glass of schnapps. Ernest Hemingway is partially responsible for this as he gave the green light for the evolution of increasingly dry martinis with his 15:1 variant. The situation was truly brought to a head by Ian Fleming when he allowed 007 to consume vodka instead of gin in this wonderfully aromatic classic.

**INGREDIENTS**
60ML (2FL OZ) TANQUERAY NO.
  TEN GIN
30ML (1FL OZ) DRY VERMOUTH
2 DASHES ORANGE BITTERS
1 SMALL PIECE LEMON ZEST
  FOR SQUEEZING

COCKTAIL GLASS

**PREPARATION**
Fill a mixing glass with ice and stir without any other ingredients. Pour off the melted water. Add gin, vermouth, and bitters and stir to chill. Strain into a pre-chilled cocktail glass and scent with the lemon zest so that the essential oils from the peel float over the surface of the drink.

An olive in the drink might be commonplace, but it really has no business there.

# GOLDEN BARTINI ON THE ROCKS

Every bar needs its "signature Martini cocktail". Our twist is based on one of the earliest mentions of the dry Martini in Thomas Stuart's mixing book from 1896; I just use Lillet Blanc instead of dry French vermouth. In the Golden Bar this is served on real "rocks", namely deep frozen pebbles from the river Isar. It doesn't matter what pebbles you choose as long as they are smooth. These keep the drink nice and cool without diluting it: because the composition is perfect just as it is straight from the mixing glass.

**INGREDIENTS**
60ML (2FL OZ) TANQUERAY NO. TEN GIN
30ML (1FL OZ) LILLET BLANC
2 DASHES ORANGE BITTERS
1 SMALL PIECE LEMON ZEST FOR SQUEEZING
FROZEN SMOOTH PEBBLES

OLD FASHIONED GLASS

**PREPARATION**
Stir all the ingredients 72 times in a mixing glass with double frozen ice cubes and pour into the Old Fashioned glass with the frozen pebbles. Add the scent of a little piece of lemon zest, but don't put the whole zest into the drink.

Clean the stones in the dishwasher and deep-freeze them at –18°C (–0.4°F) in the freezer.

# CHAMPAGNE COCKTAIL

This all-time classic gets an early mention in Jerry Thomas' *How to Mix Drinks, or the Bon Vivant's Companion* from 1862. In those days, the champagne cocktail was often also served with Cognac – which, though a perfect combination, turns this gentle beverage into a dangerous weapon. Traditionally the cocktail also has lemon zest squeezed over it (see p.26), whereby the lemon oils lie on the upper surface giving the drink a wonderfully fresh aroma. Unfortunately the oils destroy the champagne's perlage, which is what prompted me to impart the lemon flavours by means of the sugar cube.

### INGREDIENTS
1 SUGAR CUBE
1 ORGANIC LEMON
SEXY BITTERS OR OTHER
  BITTERS
20ML (¾FL OZ) COGNAC (TO
  TASTE)
1 GLASS PERRIER JOUËT GRAND
  BRUT CHAMPAGNE

CHAMPAGNE FLUTE

### PREPARATION
Rub the sugar cube thoroughly on all sides over the lemon peel to flavour it. Then soak it in the bitters and add it to the glass. If you wish, pour over 20ml (¾fl oz) good-quality Cognac. Carefully top up with chilled champagne. Do not stir! The drink is dry to start with and by the end becomes stronger and sweeter. The final swig is aromatic and sweet.

An interesting alternative: instead of serving it as a cocktail, serve the champagne neat alongside home-made Angostura marshmallows (see p.152).

# FROZEN SAZERAC

Treat yourself to this summer pleasure! Nearly every dry classic can be converted into a frozen drink using this method. Just make sure you use more syrup than specified in the original recipe. If you are using an ice-slush machine, the same quantities of water and alcohol should be used because otherwise the drink will be too strong and is likely to have an overwhelming impact…

### INGREDIENTS

50ML (1¾FL OZ) BULLEIT RYE
   WHISKY
20ML (¾FL OZ) SUGAR SYRUP
   (SEE P.158)
1 TSP ABSINTHE, SUCH AS
   DUPLAIS VERTE
5 DASHES PEYCHAUD'S BITTERS
1 DASH ANGOSTURA BITTERS

### LONG DRINK GLASS

### PREPARATION

Mix all the ingredients with a portion of crushed ice (one full glass) in an electronic mixer and pour into a long drink glass. If you would like to make the drink in an ice-slush machine, replace the ice with 50ml (1¾fl oz) still water and process the ingredients until the consistency is half frozen and slushy.

### TRY OUT THESE SUMMER HIGHLIGHTS TOO:

### FROZEN GIN AND TONIC:
traditionally or, alternatively, try with sloe gin (see p.162) or a cold drip (with beetroot, hibiscus, or nettles, see p.163).

### FROZEN VERMOUTH AND TONIC:
aromatic and somewhat lighter than with gin.

Serve with a straw and enjoy with caution as you barely taste the alcohol, but you'll soon feel its effects!

# PINK GIN NO. TEN

In its day pink gin was drunk aboard British navy ships. Alcohol was used medicinally to combat infectious diseases and so gin was a fundamental component in any ship's galley. Since it usually had a higher percentage alcohol content than today it would have been diluted 1:1 with cold water. Peak flavour and aromas for a spirit are usually experienced at around 25 per cent alcohol content. I recommend this drink not for medicinal purposes, but because it provides a pleasurable opportunity to try new varieties of gin. More variations can be produced if you try out various bitters; their spicy notes help round off the flavour.

**INGREDIENTS**
50ML (1¾FL OZ) ICE COLD TANQUERAY NO. TEN
50ML (1¾FL OZ) ICE COLD STILL WATER
5 DASHES SEXY BITTERS OR OTHER BITTERS

**LARGE WINE GLASS**

**PREPARATION**
Chill the gin in the freezer at –18°C (–4°F). Rinse out the wine glass with a couple of ice cubes. Tip the melt water away and add 5 dashes of bitters to the glass. Tilt and turn until the glass is thoroughly moistened on the inside. At this stage, I recommend smelling deep down inside the glass. Pour in the ice cold gin, swill round again, and smell once more. Add the iced water, swill briefly, and enjoy.

**Adding water to the spirit is the best way of judging its quality.**

84

# FRENCH DAISY

The Daisy is a mutation of the Sour and came about around the middle of the 19th century. Originally it was part of the triumvirate of drinks, along with the Fizz and the Collins, which were made up with soda. The "old school" Daisy turns up for the first time in Jerry Thomas' *How to Mix Drinks* from 1876. It consisted of spirit, lemon, and orange cordial and was served in a small beaker with a shot of soda. Later on larger glasses were used, the liqueur was replaced by gaudy syrups, and decorations were added using anything the fruit bowl could provide. A proper fancy drink, which is well worth rediscovering.

**INGREDIENTS**
60ML (2FL OZ) COGNAC V.S.O.P.
20ML (¾FL OZ) YELLOW
  CHARTREUSE
20ML (¾FL OZ) FRESH LEMON
  JUICE
1 BSP ABSINTHE, SUCH AS
  DUPLAIS VERTE
1 BSP SUGAR SYRUP (SEE P.158)
A TOUCH OF SODA
FRESH MINT
SLICE OF LEMON
SEASONAL FRUITS

**LARGE WINE GLASS**

**PREPARATION**
Stir all the ingredients except the soda in a mixing glass with crushed ice. Fill a red wine glass with freshly crushed ice and strain the drink into the glass. Top up with a shot of soda and, if necessary, some additional crushed ice until it is filled to over the brim. Decorate with a sprig of mint, lemon slice, and some seasonal fruits.

It's fine to use a straw for drinks on crushed ice. With other types of drink, though, you should do without.

# OLD FASHIONED

Although simplistic in its construction, when this drink is skilfully prepared it is a stunner and also a bartender's favourite. The Old Fashioned doesn't show up on drink menus until the end of the 19th century, but the first time cocktails are written about, in *The Balance and Columbian Repository*, 1806, comes very close to a description of it. A letter from a reader is answered as follows: "A cocktail, then, is a stimulating liquor, composed of any kind of spirit, sugar, and bitters …" You can use any good-quality spirit for this classic drink, and then vary it in all sorts of ways with your choice of additional ingredients.

**INGREDIENTS**
1 SUGAR CUBE
ANGOSTURA BITTERS
60ML (2FL OZ) BOURBON OR RYE
  WHISKY
1 PIECE ORANGE ZEST FOR
  SQUEEZING

**OLD FASHIONED GLASS**

**PREPARATION**
Soak the sugar cube in the bitters and add to the glass. Pour in the whisky and crush the sugar with the end of a spoon until it dissolves. Fill the glass with ice and stir until the ice melts a little. Top up with ice again, stir, and repeat until the glass is filled with liquid to 1cm (½in) below the rim. Squeeze over the orange zest.

On no account taint your Old Fashioned with the addition of cherries or other fruits. This is not a fruit salad!

# ZACHARIAS

Use your favourite malt whisky for this wonderfully fruity variation on the Old Fashioned. Home-made malt beer syrup serves as a sweetener, perfectly supporting any single malt with its flavours. The interplay between the powerful malty flavours of the drink on your palate and the fruitiness of the foam on your lips is unbelievably thrilling.

**INGREDIENTS**

50ML (1¾FL OZ) SINGLE MALT
  WHISKY
1 TSP MALT BEER SYRUP
  (SEE P.160)
2 DASHES SEXY BITTERS
CREAMY ORANGE FOAM
  (SEE P.162)

**OLD FASHIONED GLASS**

**PREPARATION**

Place the whisky, syrup, and bitters in the glass and stir gently. Add the ice and stir until melt water is produced and the ice gradually clings to the glass. Add more ice and stir again until the ice and liquid are around a finger's width below the rim of the glass. Then spray on the foam up to the brim and serve with a smile.

Try different single malts to experience how versatile this drink can be.

# DIRTY OLD BASTARD

The Dirty Old Bastard is a variant on the Old Fashioned that lives up to its name. Powerful, smoky, and spicy, this masculine creation of mine is characterized by its long and slightly sharp finish. The smoky flavours of the whisky and lapsang souchong tea go wonderfully well with the sweet spicy notes of the bitters and the added bite of the chilli. Best served with a glass of iced water alongside.

**INGREDIENTS**
1 VERY SMALL PIECE DESEEDED
   RED CHILLI PEPPER, OR
   SRIRACHA HOT CHILLI SAUCE
2 TSP LAPSANG SOUCHONG
   SYRUP (SEE P.160)
A FEW DASHES SEXY BITTERS
50ML (1¾FL OZ) ARDBEG TEN
   SINGLE MALT WHISKY

OLD FASHIONED GLASS

**PREPARATION**
Place the chilli pepper in the glass and press lightly. If you are using hot chilli sauce, add a 1cm (½in) long strip on the base of the glass. Pour over the tea syrup and a couple of dashes of the bitters and stir. Add the whisky and stir once again. Next, gradually add the ice and continue stirring and adding ice until the glass is filled to just below the rim with ice and liquid.

Lapsang souchong tea is smoked over oak chippings, making it the perfect partner for a single malt whisky from Islay.

# THE BICHLMAIER

Our head bartender Maximilian Hildebrandt created this outstanding twist for the classic Old Fashioned or the legendary Padovani. He uses home-made elderflower syrup, but high-quality shop-bought syrup will work just as well. Kilchoman, a very young, aromatic, and strong Islay single malt, lends the drink a distinctively peaty and smoky background flavour, which combines beautifully with the delicately bitter camomile of the OK drops (see p.15). A really complex and powerful drink with depth.

**INGREDIENTS**
50ML (1¾FL OZ) BULLEIT RYE
  WHISKY
20ML (¾FL OZ) ELDERFLOWER
  SYRUP (SEE P.159)
3 DASHES OK DROPS
1 DASH SINGLE MALT WHISKY,
  SUCH AS KILCHOMAN

**OLD FASHIONED GLASSD**

**PREPARATION**
Stir the rye whisky, syrup, and bitters with a hand-carved ice ball (spherical ice cube) or a large chunk of ice for 1 minute using a long-stemmed bar spoon. Add a couple of drops of single malt whisky and serve. Instead of Kilchoman you can also use any other strong, peaty single malt.

**Melt water gives a drink complexity and a perfect viscosity, and facilitates perception of aromas and flavours.**

# VANILLA PUNCH

This drink can be found in the very first edition of Jerry Thomas' cocktails book *How to Mix Drinks* from 1862. To intensify the vanilla flavours a bit more I add a small shot of vanilla liqueur. Alternatively, you could use a home-made vanilla syrup, which is really easy to prepare (see below).

**INGREDIENTS**
50ML (1¾FL OZ) COGNAC V.S.O.P.
30ML (1FL OZ) FRESH LEMON
 JUICE
2 TSP VANILLA LIQUEUR, SUCH
 AS GIFFARD VANILLE DE
 MADAGASCAR
2 BSP VANILLA SUGAR

**SMALL BEAKER**

**PREPARATION**
Vigorously shake all the ingredients in a shaker with solid ice and strain into a tumbler filled with crushed ice. Top up with some more crushed ice and, if desired, garnish with a little piece of vanilla pod.

## VANILLA SYRUP

**INGREDIENTS**
1 LITRE (1¾ PINTS) SUGAR
 SYRUP (SEE P.158)
3 GOOD-QUALITY VANILLA PODS

**PREPARATION**
Pour the sugar syrup into a bottle. Cut the vanilla pods lengthways, add to the bottle, and store in a cool, dark place. The syrup is ready for use after 24 hours.

## VANILLA SUGAR

**INGREDIENTS**
500G (1LB 2OZ) ICING SUGAR
2 GOOD-QUALITY VANILLA PODS

**PREPARATION**
Place the sugar in a jar with two vanilla pods that have been sliced open and seal the lid. Leave the flavours to develop for 2 days, shaking it occasionally during this time.

# OLD MCCARTHY

Intended for all you fans of twists on the Manhattan: here comes another one! There's hardly another classic that has produced more stories or variations. The one thing for sure is that the Manhattan first emerged in New York's dimly lit bars towards the end of the 19th century. Some say it was first ordered in 1874 in a bar in New York City by Jennie Churchill, mother of the future British prime minister. I think that this was simply one version of the then popular vermouth cocktail, which was pepped up a bit with the addition of a generous portion of whisky.

### INGREDIENTS
40ML (1¼FL OZ) BULLEIT RYE
 WHISKY
20ML (¾FL OZ) CARPANO
 ANTICA FORMULA VERMOUTH
20ML (¾FL OZ) YELLOW
 CHARTREUSE
20ML (¾FL OZ) PLUM BRANDY
1 PIECE ORANGE ZEST FOR
 SQUEEZING

### COCKTAIL GLASS

### PREPARATION
Stir all the ingredients in a mixing glass with plenty of ice for around 10–15 seconds, then strain into a pre-chilled cocktail glass. Add the scent of a little bit of orange zest and serve.

**Always keep vermouth chilled once open and use quickly. It does keep, but not indefinitely.**

# CORN 'N' OIL

The people of Barbados and Jamaica are particularly fond of this wonderfully strong rum drink. It is similar to the Petit Punch that is still popular in the Caribbean, in which white rum, fresh lime, and sugar are quite simply mixed with ice in a small beaker. Corn 'n' Oil gets its name from the oily consistency of the syrupy falernum, which spreads over the ice cubes as you prepare the drink. The sweetness can be adjusted to taste. Some people even mix the rum and syrup in a ratio of 1:2. The beverage gets a touch of freshness from 1–2 squeezes of lime, while the aromatic bitters ensure the necessary depth of flavour.

**INGREDIENTS**
1 TBSP FALERNUM (SEE P.159)
50ML (1¾FL OZ) GOOD DARK
  RUM
1 TBSP FRESH LIME JUICE
2 DASHES SEXY BITTERS OR
  AROMATIC BITTERS (P. 156)
1–2 SQUEEZES FRESH LIME

**LARGE TUMBLER**

**PREPARATION**
Place large ice cubes in the tumbler and pour the falernum over. Next add rum, lime juice, and bitters and stir the drink until it is cold. Finally, top up with more ice and finish off with 1–2 squeezes of lime.

A Petit Punch is an undoubtedly finer alternative to the Caipirinha, Brazil's national cocktail.

# RUFFTIME MARGARITA

The justifiably much loved Margarita is first mentioned in writing in 1937 in the *Café Royal Cocktail Book* under the name Toreador. But its origin, in my opinion, is simply a tequila version of the then popular Daisy. In my version, mezcal gives the recipe more depth and a slightly smoky flavour. In addition, a mixture of orange Curaçao and agave syrup brings a very interesting and broad sweetness to the palate. A further twist is provided by the cinnamon and salt mix for the crusta.

**INGREDIENTS**
1 BSP CINNAMON
1 BSP SEA SALT, SUCH AS FLEUR DE SEL
1 ORGANIC LIME
60ML (2FL OZ) MEZCAL
30ML (1FL OZ) FRESH LIME JUICE
20ML (¾FL OZ) AGAVE SYRUP
1 TSP ORANGE CURAÇAO

**COCKTAIL GLASS**

**PREPARATION**
Blend the cinnamon and salt in a mortar. Cut the lime and gently moisten the outer rim of the cocktail glass with the cut surface of the lime before dipping it into the salt and cinnamon mixture to create a delicate crust. Vigorously shake all the other ingredients with solid ice in a shaker and double strain into the glass.

Using agave syrup instead of orange Curaçao makes a margarita that can be more easily tolerated by diabetics.

# CRUSTAFARAI

Anton Utin, Maître D' of the Golden Bar, got the idea for this creation from Charles H. Baker's magnificent *The Gentleman's Companion* from 1946. Crustas, which are highly fruity beverages based on a wide variety of alcohols with aromatic ingredients and a thick sugar edging around the glass (crusta), were an obligatory component on every good drinks menu in those days. They were particularly popular as a refreshing concoction, which could be enjoyed both day and night. The Crustafarai is dedicated to Jamaica and, with this in mind, we hunted out a renowned, very crisp and honest rum blend from the island.

**INGREDIENTS**
1 ORGANIC LIME
FINE WHITE CANE SUGAR
60ML (2FL OZ) MYERS'S RUM
30ML (1FL OZ) FRESH LIME JUICE
2TSP FALERNUM (SEE P.159)
1 TSP MARASCHINO LUXARDO
1 TSP STONE'S GINGER WINE
3 DASHES SEXY BITTERS

LARGE BRANDY BALLOON
GLASS OR TUMBLER

**PREPARATION**
Peel the lime all around to make a long strip of zest. Now cut the fruit and moisten the rim of the glass with the cut surface before dipping it deep enough into a bowl of cane sugar to make a crusta around 2cm (¾in) wide. Line the inside of the glass with the lime zest strip and fill with large ice cubes. Place all the other ingredients in the shaker and shake vigorously along with some solid ice. Strain the drink into the glass and serve.

# RASTA NAIL

This simple twist is a variant on the well-known Rusty Nail which, in the original version, consists of Scotch whisky and Drambuie, a Scottish whisky with herbs and honey. For me, the bread and butter of every drink is simply to take two good-quality ingredients and that's it – no bells and whistles, no decorations. Instead of coffee liqueur I use home-made agave coffee. It is far more aromatic, has a lovely depth, and tastes like fresh, good-quality coffee. In comparison to liqueur, which is sweetened with at least 200g (7oz) of sugar per litre, here just small quantities of rock candy syrup suffice as a sweetener.

**INGREDIENTS**
40ML (1¼FL OZ) DARK MATURE
  JAMAICAN RUM
30ML (1FL OZ) HOME-MADE
  AGAVE COFFEE OR TIA MARIA
  COFFEE LIQUEUR

OLD FASHIONED GLASS

**PREPARATION**
Stir both the ingredients with some large ice cubes in the glass and serve.

## HOME-MADE AGAVE COFFEE

**INGREDIENTS**
80G (2¾OZ) COFFEE, FRESHLY
  GROUND, 100% ARABICA FROM
  GUATEMALA OR MEXICO
1 BOTTLE TEQUILA (700ML/1¼
  PINTS)
20–40ML (¾– 1¼FL OZ) ROCK
  CANDY SYRUP (SEE P.160)

**PREPARATION**
Pour coffee into the filter chamber of a cold dripper (see p.12). Moisten with tequila and pour the rest of the bottle into the water container. Set the drip rate to 2 seconds per drop. After 24 hours sweeten with rock candy syrup (quantity according to taste).

# YELLOW SMASH

A "smash" is an old category of drink that is related to the sours. Spirits, fresh herbs, and sweet and sour ingredients are shaken vigorously before being strained onto ice in an Old Fashioned glass or (without ice) into a sherry glass. To make sure that the little pieces of leaves that are produced during shaking don't end up in the drink, the double straining or fine straining technique is used (see p.26). If you serve the drink on ice you can add an aromatic decoration in the form of a pretty sprig or little bouquet of the herbs you used.

**INGREDIENTS**
60ML (2FL OZ) YELLOW
  CHARTREUSE
1 HANDFUL FRESH MINT LEAVES
30ML (1FL OZ) FRESH LIME JUICE
2 DASHES ORANGE CURAÇAO
2 DASHES SUGAR SYRUP
  (SEE P. 158)
FRESH MINT FOR DECORATING

OLD FASHIONED

**PREPARATION**
Shake all the ingredients with solid ice very vigorously for around 15 seconds in the shaker and fine strain into a glass filled with crushed ice. Garnish with a little bouquet of mint.

Before using the herbs, "bruise" them (see p.110) to release the essential oils.

# RASPBERRY RUM SMASH

Our version of the smash with its fresh raspberry purée is particularly popular with female guests at the Golden Bar. The drink is even more aromatic and intense in flavour when "bruised" herbs are added. This is achieved by taking the mint in the palm of your hand and clapping your hands together. The air pressure causes the capillaries in the leaves where the essential oils are located to open up, which greatly intensifies the smell and taste of the herbs. With herbs that you wish to use decoratively you will need to be a bit gentler and clap with your hands hollowed out so that the leaves retain their shape beautifully.

**INGREDIENTS**
50ML (1¾FL OZ) DARK RUM
2TSP CHAMBORD BERRY
  LIQUEUR
1 HANDFUL FRESH MINT LEAVES
30ML (1FL OZ) FRESH LEMON
  JUICE
30ML (1FL OZ) FRESH
  RASPBERRY PURÉE
20ML (¾FL OZ) RASPBERRY
  SYRUP (SEE P.159)
FRESH MINT FOR DECORATING

**OLD FASHIONED GLASS**

**PREPARATION**
Vigorously shake all the ingredients with solid ice in the shaker for around 15 seconds and double strain into a glass filled with crushed ice. Garnish with a pretty mint bouquet.

# ARDBEG JULEP

The julep is one of the oldest drinks in the history of the cocktail. It was around as early as the 18th century in the southern states of the USA, prepared with American whisky or brandy and particularly enjoyed as an after-breakfast drink. My powerfully aromatic version with its peaty Islay single malt is most definitely not something for the morning. Nonetheless, it is characterized by an incredible freshness and a hint of lavender, which you see and smell continuously in Scotland as you travel around the country.

**INGREDIENTS**
60ML (2FL OZ) ARDBEG TEN
  SINGLE MALT WHISKY
2TSP SUGAR SYRUP (SEE P.158)
1 HANDFUL FRESH MINT LEAVES
LAVENDER BLOSSOM FOR
  DECORATING, DRIED OR FRESH

**SILVER GOBLET OR**
**GLASS BEAKER**

**PREPARATION**
Stir the whisky and sugar syrup together with a handful of bruised mint leaves (see p.110) in a silver goblet or glass. Top up with crushed ice and stir vigorously to produce melt water and to cool the drink. Top up with crushed ice once again and decorate with a bouquet of lavender blossom. Serve with a straw.

Cut the straw short enough so that your nose can detect the aroma of the herbs while you're drinking.

# CHOCOLATE COCKTAIL

Harry Johnson's sweet delicacy is to be found in his *Bartender's Manual* from 1900. This book is one of the most important in the history of the cocktail and shows how, even more than a 100 years ago, there was some really creative mixing going on. Harry Johnson was of German extraction and worked as a bartender in New York City. For many of his drinks he used yellow Chartreuse as a source of sweetness: my kind of guy! The following concoction is the only really sweet recipe in this book and is also perfectly suited as a dessert.

**INGREDIENTS**
40ML (1¼FL OZ) LBV PORT
40ML (1¼FL OZ) YELLOW
  CHARTREUSE
1 FRESH EGG YOLK
1 BSP COCOA POWDER
NUTMEG TO GARNISH

**COCKTAIL GLASS**

**PREPARATION**
Vigorously shake all the ingredients with solid ice for 10–15 seconds in a shaker and double strain into a pre-chilled cocktail glass. Freshly grate over a sprinkle of nutmeg and drink up quickly.

Nutmeg is one of the oldest adornments for a cocktail: inexpensive, highly aromatic, and, in higher doses, intoxicating but also poisonous.

# BLOODY GEISHA

At the start of the 20th century in Harry's New York Bar in Paris the Bloody Mary was still known as the Red Snapper, but it was already being mixed entirely in the classic style with gin, Worcestershire sauce, Tabasco, celery salt, and a slug of lemon juice. Whether it's a Mary or a Geisha – the important thing is not to use too much alcohol or to over-dilute the mixture. For the Red Snapper I use 20–30ml (¾–1fl oz) gin and make the drink with well-chilled ingredients in a pre-chilled glass without any ice. An exceptionally delicious alternative is the Pechuga Mary, made with Mezcal de Pechuga (see p.16), grilled lime juice (see p.54), and hot chilli sauce. In the Golden Bar we serve this with a Parma ham crisp.

**INGREDIENTS**

40ML (1¼FL OZ) DAIGINJO SAKE

140ML (4¾FL OZ) FINEST
   TOMATO JUICE

1 SQUEEZE FRESH LIME

2 DASHES CASK AGED SOY
   SAUCE

1–2 BSP KIZAMI WASABI
   (PURÉED FRESH WASABI)

1 SMALL PINCH SEA SALT, SUCH
   AS FLEUR DE SEL

FRESHLY GROUND BLACK
   PEPPER, TO GARNISH

**SMALL BEAKER**

**PREPARATION**

Pre-chill the beaker. Place the ingredients in the shaker. Cool the drink down by shaking everything back and forth 3–4 times between two shakers, one of which is filled with ice and covered with a cocktail filter. This technique is known as "throwing". Alternatively, stir the ingredients gently for a few seconds with some ice. Strain into the glass and garnish with a pinch of pepper.

An ideal hangover beverage: vitamins, protein, and electrolytes will help get you back on your feet.

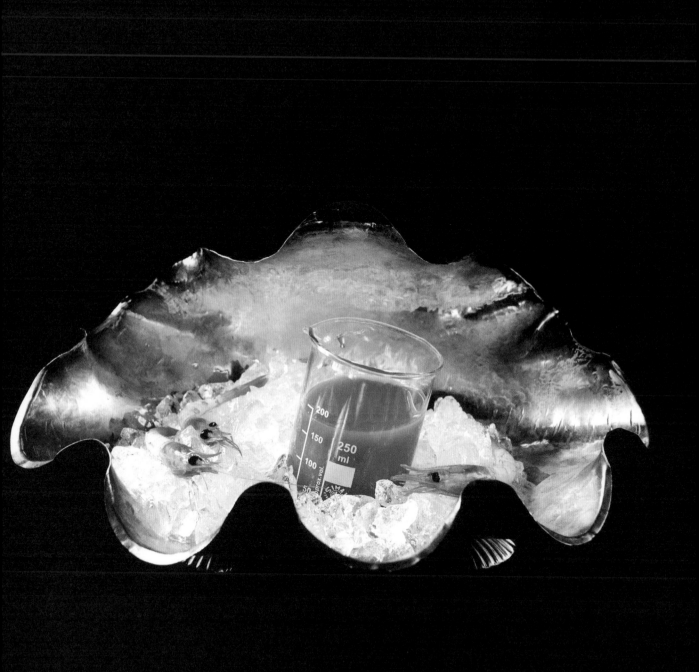

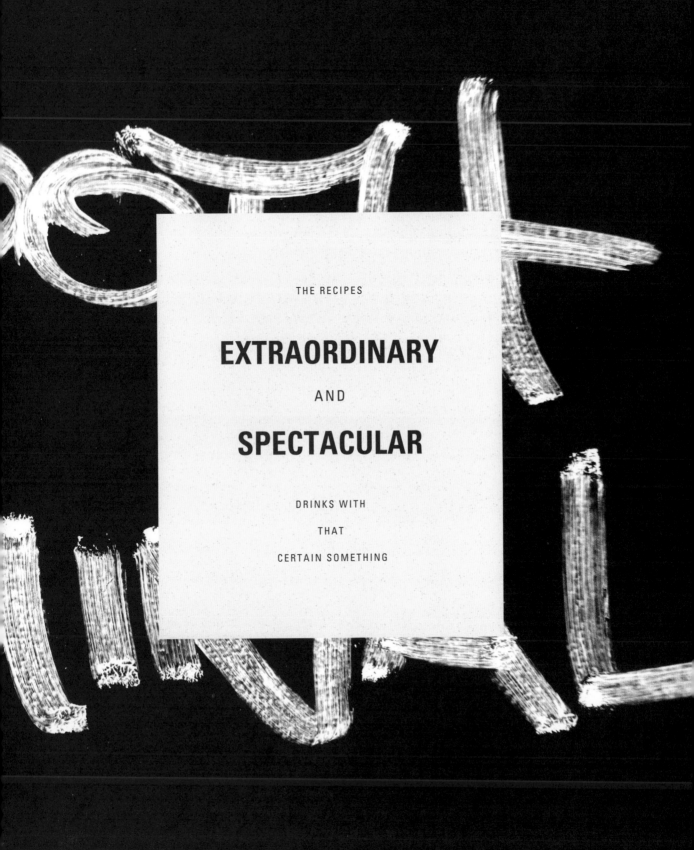

THE RECIPES

# EXTRAORDINARY

## AND

# SPECTACULAR

DRINKS WITH

THAT

CERTAIN SOMETHING

# HAUS DER KUNST COCKTAIL

This is my own creation, which I have dedicated to the Haus der Kunst ("House of Art") museum in Munich where the Golden Bar is located. The modern artistic transformation of the bar with works by Florian Süssmayr offers a stimulating contrast to the very classical museum space. That's how the drink should be, too. It is based on the French 75, a champagne cocktail with gin, sugar, and lemon, which is first mentioned by Harry Craddock in 1930 in *The Savoy Cocktail Book*. It is served on large ice cubes in an Old Fashioned glass and topped with a gin and tonic foam.

**INGREDIENTS**
50ML (1¾FL OZ) TANQUERAY NO. TEN GIN
30ML (1FL OZ) FRESH LEMON JUICE
2 BSP ICING SUGAR
PERRIER JOUËT GRAND BRUT CHAMPAGNE
GIN AND TONIC FOAM (SEE P.162)
CAMPARI DUST (SEE P.162)

**OLD FASHIONED GLASS**

**PREPARATION**
Vigorously shake together the gin, lemon juice, and sugar with solid ice and strain into an Old Fashioned glass filled with ice cubes. Top up with a bit of champagne and spray on the gin and tonic foam to crown it off. Decorate with a pinch of Campari dust.

Foams can be made in the blink of an eye and enable the creation of stunning effects when reinterpreting classic drinks.

# ROYAL CAMOMILE TEA

A little twist dresses up the ever familiar mojito in some new floral garb. The camomile syrup can be made in an instant so this exceptional drink is really easy to prepare. What's more, you can easily create your own variations on the mojito by making a sugar syrup using the herbs, fruit, or spices of your choice then incorporating these decoratively in the drink as well. Normally a mojito is topped up with soda – using champagne gives it a "royal" upgrade.

## INGREDIENTS

50ML (1¾FL OZ) WHITE HAVANA CLUB 3 YEAR OLD RUM
30ML (1FL OZ) FRESH LEMON JUICE
20ML (¾FL OZ) CAMOMILE SYRUP (SEE P.159)
2 DASHES OK DROPS (SEE P.15)
PERRIER JOUËT GRAND BRUT CHAMPAGNE
DRIED CAMOMILE FLOWERS

**LONG DRINK GLASS**

## PREPARATION

Place all the ingredients except the champagne and flowers in a long drink glass and stir. Fill with ice and top up with champagne. Add camomile flowers to the drink, stir gently once more, and serve.

OK drops are aromatic bitters based on camomile flowers and are available in specialist shops or online.

# BEETROOT GIMLET

The gimlet is another of those classic drinks that no bar should countenance being without. Equal parts lime juice cordial and gin combine to create a fruity and fresh beverage. I prefer to use the lime juice sparingly and to flavour only the gin. There are countless other varieties of gimlet that all work really well, such as Jeffrey Morgenthaler's Richmond Gimlet from the USA. Here is my version: with beetroot and a hint of chocolate.

## INGREDIENTS
1 ORGANIC LIME
COCOA POWDER
50ML (1¾FL OZ) BEETROOT
  COLD DRIP (SEE P.163)
30ML (1FL OZ) LIME JUICE
  CORDIAL (SEE P.160)

COCKTAIL GLASS

## PREPARATION
Moisten the rim of the cocktail glass with the cut surface of a lime and dust it upside down with cocoa powder to create a delicate chocolate border around the glass. Stir the remaining ingredients with large ice cubes in a mixing glass and strain into the cocktail glass.

You'll find combination possibilities for the most diverse flavours at www.foodpairing.com.

# SMOOTH CRIMINAL

Pretty powerful, but easy to drink – this combination makes a drink that is aptly named. The cube of fresh pineapple is the key to success as it gives the cocktail its silky consistency. Using pineapple juice as an alternative here really would be a crime.

**INGREDIENTS**

1 CUBE FRESH PINEAPPLE
 (2×2×2CM/¾×¾×¾IN)
50ML (1¾FL OZ) BULLEIT RYE
 WHISKY
2 TSP ORANGE CURAÇAO
1 TSP MARASCHINO LUXARDO
1 TSP SUGAR SYRUP (SEE P.158)
1 DASH ANGOSTURA BITTERS
PERRIER JOUËT GRAND BRUT
 CHAMPAGNE

**COCKTAIL GLASS OR
SILVER GOBLET**

**PREPARATION**

Press the pineapple cube gently in the shaker with a muddler. Add all the other ingredients and shake vigorously with solid ice. Double strain into the glass or silver goblet and top up with a generous shot of champagne.

Maraschino is
the Jedi power for
bartenders... but
you must know
how to use it.

# BLOOD AND SAND

Named after the 1922 film with Rudolph Valentino, the Blood and Sand has established itself as a perennial classic. This variant is a great twist on the original and is a powerful expression of the Golden Bar's methods and concepts. The basic ingredients are Scotch, red vermouth, cherry liqueur, and orange juice. I alter the juice at a molecular level by turning it into a light orange cream, which I then place on top of the drink. The mouthfeel is completely different and it's a superb sensation letting the drink flow over your palate below the refreshing foam.

## INGREDIENTS

30ML (1FL OZ) BLENDED SCOTCH
  WHISKY
30ML (1FL OZ) CARPANO ANTICA
  FORMULA VERMOUTH
30ML (1FL OZ) CHERRY LIQUEUR,
  SUCH AS HEERING
CREAMY ORANGE FOAM
  (SEE P.162)

OLD FASHIONED GLASS

## PREPARATION

Stir the Scotch, vermouth, and cherry liqueur with large ice cubes in an Old Fashioned glass. Top with the creamy orange foam and serve.

# MY BUCK AND BRECK

Buchanan and Breckinridge might have been the least successful government team in US history, but they also left behind a positive influence: as the namesakes for a classic drink and for my absolutely favourite bar in Berlin, which I think is one of the best in the world. While having the utmost respect for the original drink, I have allowed myself to tinker with it just a little. Instead of sugar I use a dust made from dehydrated green Chartreuse, which I fix around the rim of the glass in the form of a crusta. This means that every mouthful contains a herby-sweet interplay of flavours between the crusta and the remaining ingredients.

**INGREDIENTS**
1 SPRAY OF ABSINTHE, SUCH AS
  DUPLAIS VERTE
CHARTREUSE DUST (SEE P.162)
20ML (¾FL OZ) COGNAC V.S.O.P.
PERRIER JOUËT GRAND BRUT
  CHAMPAGNE

SILVER GOBLET

**PREPARATION**
Moisten the outer rim of the tumbler with a bit of absinthe from an atomizer and sprinkle on a roughly 1cm (½in) wide crusta from Chartreuse dust. Then spray the tumbler once more on the inside with the absinthe to add some scent. Pour in the cognac and carefully top up with champagne.

With a simple candy floss machine you can make candy floss from the Chartreuse dust and set it on top of the drink!

# NETTLE TEA

With champagne cocktails you should add a little shot of champagne to the shaker before straining. This makes the drink more homogeneous and it won't froth over when you pour it.

**INGREDIENTS**
20ML (¾FL OZ) NETTLE COLD
    DRIP (SEE P.163)
2 TSP FRESH LEMON JUICE
2 TSP RUNNY HONEY (SEE P.160)
PERRIER JOUËT GRAND BRUT
    CHAMPAGNE

CHAMPAGNE FLUTE

**PREPARATION**
Vigorously shake all the ingredients except for the champagne for a short time in the shaker with solid ice before double straining into a pre-chilled champagne flute. Top up with champagne (see picture, right).

# CARAMELLOW ROYAL

The ginger chips for this recipe can be prepared quite easily in the oven (see below).

**INGREDIENTS**
1 GINGER CHIP
1 TSP VANILLA LIQUEUR, SUCH
    AS GIFFARD VANILLE DE
    MADAGASCAR
PERRIER JOUËT GRAND BRUT
    CHAMPAGNE

CHAMPAGNE FLUTE

**PREPARATION**
Place the ginger chip in the glass and pour over the vanilla liqueur. Carefully top up with champagne and you are done.

*Ginger chips preparation: cut fresh unpeeled ginger into 2mm (¼in) thick slices, sprinkle with sugar, and leave to steep for 2 hours. Finally, bake in the oven at 160°C (325°F/ Gas 3) until crisp (see picture, left).*

# YUZU TAKETSURU

Masataka Taketsuru was the first person from Japan to learn how to distil whisky in Scotland. He brought home the knowledge he acquired in the 1920s and cultivated and perfected his skills, creating an internationally recognized style of his own: Japanese whisky. Nikka was the first Japanese distillery that Taketsuru worked for, and its From the Barrel is a wonderfully strong and aromatic whisky – exactly what this recipe requires.

**INGREDIENTS**
20ML (¾FL OZ) YUZU SAKE
50ML (1¾FL OZ) JAPANESE
  NIKKA FROM THE BARREL
  WHISKY
ONE SMALL HANDFUL FRESH
  SHISO LEAVES
1 TBSP FRESH LEMON JUICE
1 TBSP FRESH LIME JUICE
2 BSP ICING SUGAR
1 EGG WHITE
FRESH SHISO LEAVES FOR
  DECORATION

**OLD FASHIONED GLASS**

**PREPARATION**
Vigorously shake all the ingredients with solid ice in the shaker and fine strain into a glass filled with crushed ice. Garnish with shiso leaves that you have gently bruised between the palms of your hands (see p.110).

You can get fresh
shiso leaves in
Asian stores.

# ROYAL HIBISCUS GIN FIZZ

The fizz family is clearly defined. A fizz consists of a spirit, something sweet, something sour, all spritzed up with a touch of soda. If the fizz gets an additional "silver" in its name, the bartender knows that the recipe should have an egg white added. A golden fizz gets an egg yolk and a royal fizz an entire egg. This gives the drink a silky texture and the egg white also ensures a beautiful foamy crown. If the sugar is replaced by liqueur the whole thing is known as a Fix. The Royal Hibiscus Gin Fizz is an unbelievably alluring combination, which is characterized by the dry fruity notes of the hibiscus cold drip and, just for once, is served on ice in a long drink glass.

**INGREDIENTS**
50ML (1¾FL OZ) HIBISCUS COLD
   DRIP (P. 163)
1 TBSP FRESH LEMON JUICE
1 TBSP FRESH LIME JUICE
2 BSP ICING SUGAR
1 EGG
SODA FOR TOPPING UP
DRIED HIBISCUS FLOWERS FOR
   DECORATION

**LONG DRINK GLASS**

**PREPARATION**
Vigorously shake all the ingredients except the soda with solid ice in a shaker for at least 15 seconds and strain into a glass filled with ice cubes. Top up with some soda and garnish with pretty hibiscus flowers.

This drink is
also really alluring
when made with sloe
gin (see p.162).

# HOT BUTTERED COCONUT RUM

Hot Buttered Rum is a classic and in winter it is a hot favourite for general medicinal purposes. Julian Zerressen was once a mixologist at the Golden Bar and nowadays can be found behind the counter at London's renowned Happiness Forgets. He created this really interesting twist, which is far finer and more special than the original.

**INGREDIENTS**
40ML (1¼FL OZ) BANANARUMA
  (SEE P.162)
2 DASHES SEXY BITTERS
1 TBSP FALERNUM (SEE P.159)
100ML (3½FL OZ) ORGANIC
  COCONUT WATER
SPICED BUTTER (SEE P.160)
1 CINNAMON STICK FOR
  DECORATION

**SMALL BEAKER**

**PREPARATION**
Heat the bananaruma, bitters, falernum, and coconut water in a small pan to around 60–70°C (140–158°C) and pour into a small beaker. Top with a flake of spiced butter and serve with a cinnamon stick.

The steam nozzle
of an espresso machine
allows you to heat up
drinks in an instant.

# ARPI GARDENIA

This thrilling twist from our bartender Arpad Nikhazi proves that the Daisy is also at its best when combined with fresh herbs.

**INGREDIENTS**
50ML (1¾FL OZ) COGNAC V.S.O.P.
30ML (1FL OZ) FRESH LEMON
  JUICE
2 TSP DRY ORANGE CURAÇAO
2 TSP SUGAR SYRUP (SEE P.158)
2 BSP GARDENIA MIX (SEE P.160)
SODA
1 BUNCH FRESH TARRAGON

COCKTAIL GLASS

**PREPARATION**
Vigorously shake all the ingredients except the soda and herbs in a shaker with solid ice and double strain into a glass filled with crushed ice. Top with a little shot of soda and re-fill with crushed ice. Bruise the tarragon (see p.110) and add to the centre of the drink as a decoration. Serve with a straw (see picture, left).

# PHARMACY

Our head bartender Dennis Richter combines the strong flavours of a variety of liqueurs in this particularly fine and spicy variation on the well-known classic digestif, the Apothecary.

**INGREDIENTS**
20ML (¾FL OZ) MINT LIQUEUR,
  SUCH AS BRANCA MENTA
20ML (¾FL OZ) AMER PICON
  BITTER LIQUEUR
20ML (¾FL OZ) RUM LIQUEUR,
  SUCH AS THE BITTER TRUTH
  PIMENTO DRAM
20ML (¾FL OZ) LBV PORT

COCKTAIL GLASS

**PREPARATION**
Stir all the ingredients in a mixing glass together with large ice cubes and strain into a pre-chilled cocktail glass (see picture, right).

# GINTELLIGENCE NO. 2

This warming and powerful beverage is "gintelligent" and almost more of a medicine than a cocktail. Camomile calms and relaxes the muscles, while the elderflower cleanses and stimulates the body. It is especially good in winter when you come in from the chilly outdoors or if you're starting to come down with a cold: a perfect "good night cap".

**INGREDIENTS**
200ML (7FL OZ) BOTTLE EXTRA
  DRY TONIC WATER, SUCH AS
  GOLDEN MONACO
50ML (1¾FL OZ) TANQUERAY NO.
  TEN GIN
2 TSP ELDERFLOWER SYRUP
  (SEE P.159)
1 CAMOMILE TEA BAG

SILVER POT AND
LITTLE CUP OR
SILVER GOBLET

**PREPARATION**
Pre-warm the pot and cup by filling them with hot water. Heat the tonic water in a pan or with the steam nozzle of an espresso machine to just below boiling. Empty the water from the pot. Add the gin and syrup, hang the tea bag inside, and pour over the tonic water. Put the lid on and leave to draw for a few minutes. Serve in a little tea cup or silver goblet.

I recommend
Golden Monaco extra
dry tonic water because
it contains only half the
sugar compared with
many other brands.

# TWO HUNDRED

I created the Two Hundred on the occasion of the 200th edition of *GQ Magazine*. It is a variation on the well-known classic French 75, which was named after a French cannon from the First World War, no doubt also thanks to its mighty "penetrative power".

**INGREDIENTS**
1 ORGANIC LIME
HIBISCUS SUGAR (SEE P.162)
30ML (1FL OZ) HOME-MADE SLOE
  GIN (SEE P.162)
20ML (¾FL OZ) FRESH LIME
  JUICE
1 TBSP SUGAR SYRUP (SEE P.158)
PERRIER JOUËT GRAND BRUT
  CHAMPAGNE

**CHAMPAGNE FLUTE**

**PREPARATION**
Moisten the rim of the glass slightly with the cut surface of the lime and dip into the hibiscus sugar to create a delicate crusta. Vigorously shake the lime juice, sloe gin, and syrup with solid ice in a shaker, and after opening the shaker add a generous shot of champagne. Strain into the glass and top up once more with a shot of champagne.

To create a really exquisite crust, spray the glass upside down with the appropriate liqueur and then sprinkle with sugar while turning.

144

# TABULA RASA

When Giuseppe Campari first mixed his popular aperitif the Negroni in Milan the drink was still known as the Milano Torino, but it was soon renamed Americano thanks to its immense popularity among American tourists. An Americano consists of red vermouth and Campari with a little dash of soda. In the Negroni you get gin instead of soda and the Negroni Sbagliato (messed up Negroni) was invented by another bartender in Milan who inadvertently poured prosecco instead of gin into the Negroni. Whether you choose one of these variants or my own twist: this is a first-rate aperitif for the summer!

## INGREDIENTS

30ML (1FL OZ) CHOCOLATE
  SPIRIT OR CHOCOLATE LIQUOR,
  SUCH AS MOZART DRY
20ML (¾FL OZ) CAMPARI
20ML (¾FL OZ) CARPANO
  ANTICA FORMULA VERMOUTH
CREAMY ORANGE FOAM
  (SEE P.162)
CAMPARI DUST (SEE P.162)

OLD FASHIONED

## PREPARATION

Stir the liqueur, Campari, and vermouth with some ice cubes in an Old Fashioned glass. Spray on a finger's breadth of creamy orange foam and decorate with some Campari dust.

For a party drink the Americano can be carbonated in advance in a soda syphon (see p.64). Chill for 3 hours and pour into glasses with some ice.

# KRAMER'S BREAKFAST

This variation on the full Scottish breakfast was created in honour of our former colleague Claudius Kramer Brudnjak – he preferred to enjoy it of an evening rather than in the morning, and I would recommend this to you, too.

**INGREDIENTS**
15 DARK ROASTED GRAINS OF
  MALTED BARLEY
3 ARABICA COFFEE BEANS
50ML (1¾FL OZ) WHISKY, SUCH
  AS GLENLIVET NÀDURRA
1 TBSP AGAVE COFFEE
  (SEE P. 163)
2 BSP GARDENIA MIX
  (SEE P. 160)
1 BSP GRADE A MAPLE SYRUP
1 EGG YOLK

COCKTAIL GLASS

**PREPARATION**
Crush the malted barley and coffee beans in the shaker with the muddler and add all the other ingredients. Shake vigorously along with some solid ice, and double strain into a pre-chilled cocktail glass (see picture, left). Toasted white bread with some gardenia mix and roasted grains of malted barley taste delicious alongside this.

# SUBURBIA

This creation by our former bartender Oliver von Carnap is an extraordinary chorus of flavours, mixed in a spectacularly simple fashion.

**INGREDIENTS**
APRICOT BRANDY
40ML (1¼FL OZ) LBV PORT
30ML (1FL OZ) BULLEIT BOURBON
3 DASHES SEXY BITTERS
2 BSP CHERRY LIQUEUR, SUCH
  AS MARASCHINO LUXARDO

COCKTAIL GLASS

**PREPARATION**
Pour some apricot brandy into an atomizer and use this to spray the cocktail glass with the flavour. Stir all the other ingredients briefly in a mixing glass with some large ice cubes and strain into the cocktail glass (see picture, right).

# CAPTAIN STRAINER'S PLANTATION PUNCH

I recommend this tiki bowl if only because it makes such an incredible impression as an optical highlight at any chilled out cocktail party. What's more, it's easy to make even in large quantities and gets your guests in a good mood straight away. It is best not to dawdle over precise measurements, instead just use a glass (around 200ml/7fl oz) as a measuring vessel. Depending on thirst, around 10–20 people can have plenty of fun from my recipe.

## INGREDIENTS

5 CUPS PASSION FRUIT PULP
  FROM RIPE PASSION FRUIT
1 BOTTLE (700ML/1¼PINTS)
  RUM, SUCH AS HAVANA CLUB
  SELECCIÓN DE MAESTROS
2 BOTTLES (700ML/1¼PINTS)
  EXTRA AGED RUM, SUCH AS
  HAVANA CLUB 7 YEAR OLD
2 CUPS FRESH LIME JUICE
5 CUPS FRESH PINEAPPLE JUICE
3 CUPS GINGER BEER (SEE P.42)
½ CUP RUNNY HONEY (SEE P.160)
1 CUP HOME-MADE GRENADINE
  (SEE P.159)
½ CUP FALERNUM (SEE P.159)
3 CUPS LIME JUICE CORDIAL
  (SEE P.160)
33 DASHES SEXY BITTERS
FRESH FLOWERS FOR
  DECORATING

PUNCH BOWL

## PREPARATION

Prepare the punch in a large punch bowl. Halve the passion fruit and scrape out the flesh of the fruit. If you like, wash the empty halves under the tap and then use them as little cups for drinking the punch! To keep the drink cool, you should ideally use a large ice block or big chunks of ice in the centre of the bowl. Pour over all the ingredients, stir, and it's ready.

Roll the limes under the balls of your hands before pressing or squeeze them at room temperature – you will get more juice out of them this way.

# ANGOSTURA MARSHMALLOWS

Although this isn't a drink, I just couldn't deprive you of this recipe. Instead of the classic champagne cocktail, I love to serve the following fabulous alternative. Hand out an Angostura marshmallow with a glass of ice cold champagne or simply as a surprise to welcome your guests. Further interesting marshmallow variations can be created by using other bitters such as Sexy Bitters or Peychaud's Bitters instead of the Angostura. The marshmallows from this recipe will taste best on the third day, but they will keep for at least one to two weeks.

## INGREDIENTS
2 TBSP, PLUS 250G (9OZ) ICING SUGAR
2 TBSP CORNFLOUR
20G (¾OZ) LEAF GELATINE
50ML (1¾FL OZ) ANGOSTURA BITTERS
100ML (3½FL OZ) STILL WATER

## PREPARATION
Mix 2 tablespoons icing sugar and cornflour. Grease a silicon baking mould and dust with about half of this mixture. Soften the gelatine in cold water, heat the angostura and water together (do not boil!), and let the gelatine dissolve in this. Stir the mixture into 250g (9oz) icing sugar and beat with an electric whisk on the highest speed until the mixture is slightly viscous and it has approximately quadrupled in volume. Place this in the baking mould and store overnight in the fridge. The next day turn it over, dust with the icing sugar and cornflour mix, and leave to rest for a further day. Cut into little pieces and turn these in icing sugar to coat.

Angostura oral vaccination: to combat hiccups, suck on a sugar cube soaked in Angostura.

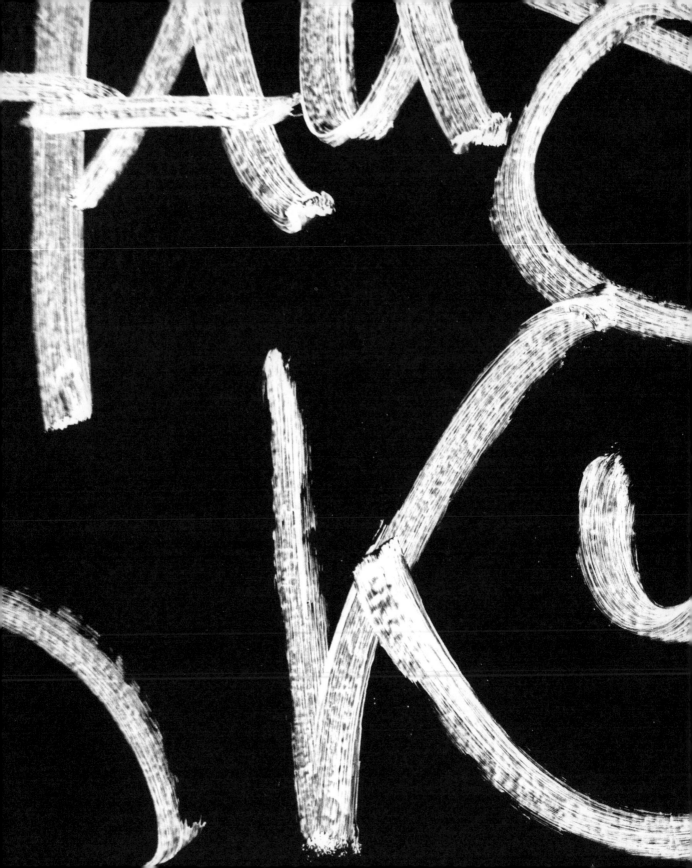

# BASIC RECIPES

AND

# ALCOHOL ABC

SIMPLE RECIPES

FOR ALL

BASIC INGREDIENTS

# AROMATIC BITTERS

**Like many other cocktail ingredients, it is quite easy to make your own aromatic bitters. Here is a basic recipe for standard aromatic bitters that are very similar to the classic Angostura bitters.**

## INGREDIENTS

8G RED SANDALWOOD POWDER
16G (½OZ) CINCHONA BARK
4G DRIED ORANGE PEEL
3G CINNAMON BARK
3G TONKA BEAN
1G STAR ANISE
1G CLOVES
900ML (1½ PINTS) VODKA (40%)
100ML (3½FL OZ) DARK RUM
50–100ML (1¾–3½FL OZ) ROCK
  CANDY SYRUP (SEE P.160)

## PREPARATION

Evenly grind the barks and spices in a food processor or using a pestle and mortar and pour over 700ml (1¼ pints) vodka. Macerate for 14 days in a sealed container (see p.163) and then strain roughly through a sieve before fine filtering through coffee filter paper. Finally add the rum, 200ml (7fl oz) vodka, and rock candy syrup (quantity according to taste) and pour into little bottles. The flavours of the bitters will become more balanced once you have stored them for a few weeks.

**You can substitute
or add ingredients
to produce your own
house bitters.**

# ADDITIONAL BASIC RECIPES

On these pages you will find instructions for the home-made ingredients used in the book. The syrup recipes can be made on the stove in a small saucepan, but it's also worth trying out the techniques below, as these will enable you to achieve even better results from a taste point of view.

### SOUS VIDE

No longer a kitchen novelty, sous vide produces great results when making syrup. Ingredients retain their flavour by cooking them in a vacuum pouch and at a low temperature. What's more, this technique prevents fruit syrups from going cloudy. If you don't own a sous vide device, you can cook heat-resistant vacuum pouches at 60°C (140°F) in your dishwasher.

### QUICK INFUSION UNDER PRESSURE

With the "quick method" the sugar syrup is put into a device known as a whipping syphon along with the herbs or spices, and then 2 nitrous oxide cartridges are inserted. The nitrogen dissolves in the liquid and penetrates the cell walls of the ingredients. After just one minute you can carefully release the gas from the syphon, which must be standing upright at this point, whereby the nitrogen bubbles out of the ingredients' cell walls and consequently imbues the liquid with an incredible flavour. Filter and it's ready!

### DEEP FREEZING

Syrups made with delicate and aromatic herbs such as basil are best made by filling a vacuum pouch with the relevant herb and adding the sugar syrup to this. Vacuum seal and store overnight in the freezer, then defrost and filter. The results are very delicate, but also wonderfully aromatic.

### SUGAR SYRUP

When I refer to sugar syrup (simple syrup) I always mean a ratio of 1:1 white sugar to water, so for example 500g (1lb 2oz) sugar to 500ml (16fl oz) water. If a strong syrup (rich syrup) is required, the ratio is 2:1, and in a light sugar syrup 1:2.

*Preparation:* bring the water and sugar to the boil until the sugar has completely dissolved. Leave to cool, decant into a clean bottle, and store in the fridge. Sugar syrup can also be produced without heating by simply leaving the mixture at room temperature and occasionally stirring with a balloon whisk. After 30–60 minutes the syrup will be clear. You can significantly extend the shelf life of any syrup by adding a tablespoon of vodka. Normal sugar syrup should keep a good month in the fridge, and with a little shot of vodka it will keep for up to three months; syrup that has been prepared without heating, however, lasts for considerably less time.

## FALERNUM

This is a kind of rum and spice syrup that is essential for many tiki drinks.

*Ingredients:* 1 cinnamon stick, 8 coffee beans, 4 cardamom pods, 6 allspice berries, 2 pieces star anise, ½ tonka bean (grated), ¼ nutmeg (grated), 2 finely chopped vanilla pods, 1 pinch sea salt (such as fleur de sel) 1 pinch black pepper, 200g (7oz) peeled finely chopped ginger, zest from 2 organic lemons and 2 organic oranges, 600ml (1 pint) Myers's rum, 600ml (1 pint) water, 1kg (2¼lb) sugar.

*Preparation:* grind all the spices with a pestle and mortar or pulse briefly in a food processor. Toast the spices, citrus zest, and ginger in a pan over a moderate heat then add the sugar and caramelize. Carefully quench with rum and water and leave to simmer for around 10 minutes. Leave to cool, then filter through a fine sieve. Pour into a clean bottle and store cold.

## GRENADINE SYRUP

Making grenadine from fresh pomegranates isn't worth the effort. The result has a very short shelf life and its colour produces rather brown drinks. *My tip:* buy a good brand of pomegranate juice and blend 1:1 with white sugar. Reduce the juice in a microwave on a moderate power setting until it is reduced by half. Stop and stir every so often to completely dissolve the sugar. You will be thrilled! Test and add sugar to taste. The syrup should have a lovely balance between sweetness and acidity.

## RASPBERRY SYRUP

Gently simmer 750g (1lb 10oz) fresh raspberries for 20 minutes with sugar syrup. Once cool, filter, decant into a clean bottle, and store in the fridge. The sous vide method is recommended here.

## ELDERFLOWER SYRUP

Take 100g (3½oz) fresh, clean elderflower heads and bring to the boil with 1 litre (1¾ pints) water, the zest of an organic lime, and 500g (1lb 2oz) sugar. Remove from the hob and stir in 15g (½oz) ascorbic acid to make the syrup last longer. Store in a cool place for 24 hours and then strain through some coffee filter paper. Decant into a clean bottle and store in the fridge.

## CAMOMILE SYRUP

Bring 500ml (16fl oz) water to the boil with 500g (1lb 2oz) sugar until the sugar has dissolved. Add 3 heaped tablespoons dried camomile flowers and leave to infuse for 20 minutes without boiling. Strain, decant into a clean bottle, and store in the fridge. Again the sous vide method is recommended here as it results in fewer bitter substances being dissolved. The freezer or quick infusion method also work well.

## PEPPERMINT SYRUP

To give a julep a bit of a boost, I like to use a little shot of light peppermint syrup. The deep freeze method words best here: simply take a bunch of fresh mint and freeze for 24 hours with 1 litre (1¾ pints) sugar syrup, then thaw and filter.

## LAPSANG SOUCHONG SYRUP

Boil up 500g (1lb 2oz) sugar with 500ml (16fl oz) water, remove from the hob, and stir in 2 tablespoons lapsang souchong tea. Leave to infuse for 10 minutes, filter into a clean bottle, and store in the fridge. The syrup also produces an exquisite iced tea: make some strong tea and add syrup, ice cubes, a splash of water, and a couple of slices and some juice from an orange and a lemon.

## LIME JUICE CORDIAL

Bring to the boil 1 litre (1¾ pints) sugar syrup with 250ml (9fl oz) freshly squeezed lime juice and the zest of 4 organic limes and leave to infuse for 15 minutes. Cool, strain, and store in a clean bottle in the fridge.

## MALT BEER SYRUP

Bring 500ml (16fl oz) non-alcoholic malt beer to the boil with 500g (1lb 2oz) light muscovado sugar, and simmer gently until the liquid has reduced by around a half.

## ROCK CANDY SYRUP

Heat rock candy (rock sugar) and water in a ratio of 1:1 in a saucepan until the sugar has completely dissolved. Pour into a clean bottle and store in the fridge. I particularly like to use this syrup as a sweetener for macerations, for example, in the agave coffee (see p.163).

## RUNNY HONEY

This is the answer if you want to mix drinks with honey – it often lends more depth and texture to a drink than sugar syrup, but it is difficult to dissolve in cold ingredients. *Preparation*: stir 2 parts honey together with 1 part hot water until the honey has completely liquefied. It remains liquid even if you put the mixture into a clean bottle and store in the fridge.

## TRIPLE SYRUP

This is similarly a secret weapon for adding a bit more depth and complexity to drinks. Blend equal parts sugar syrup, runny honey, and agave syrup, then decant into a clean bottle. Often a little dash of this is all it takes to round off a drink perfectly.

## GARDENIA MIX

This consists of honey and butter in equal proportions. Heat honey in a pan to liquefy it before adding the butter and whisking the mixture until smooth using a balloon whisk. Pour into a clean jar with a lid and store in the fridge. Allow to soften a little at room temperature before use.

## SPICE BUTTER

In a food processor, finely grind 1 tablespoon each of cocoa powder, ground coffee, and ground cinnamon with 1 star anise, 3 cloves, and 2 cardamom pods and stir into 100g (3½oz) soft butter. Leave the mixture to infuse for one day in the fridge, allow to soften at room temperature, and press through a fine mesh sieve. Shape the resulting mixture and store in the fridge.

A NOT TOO DRY TEXT BOOK
TO THE MINUTE CONNOISSEUR
COCKTAIL RECIPES
THE ART OF
MIXIN
CUPS
AND
THEIR CUSTOMS.
GIGGLE WATER
HOW
JERRY TH
CONTAININ
RECEIPTS FOR
ALL KINDS
PUNCH
EGGNOG
JULEPS
American

## DUST

This is a dried ingredient that is ground to a fine powder. By following the recipe here you can make dusts such as Campari dust (see p.120 & p.146) or Chartreuse dust (see p.130). Pour 350ml (12fl oz) of the spirit into a plastic baking mould and allow to dry for 1–2 days at 60–70°C (140–158°F) in a dehydrator (see p.12). The liquid and the alcohol will evaporate leaving behind sugar crystals, which taste clearly of the alcohol. Use a pestle and mortar to grind the crystals fairly finely, and store in a dry container in a cool place. You can also make dust in the oven. Leave the oven door open very slightly for a 2–3 day drying period so that the alcohol vapour can escape.

## HIBISCUS SUGAR

Place a few dried hibiscus flowers and some fine white sugar in an electric food processor and mix for a couple of seconds. The result is a light pink coloured sugar with dark red reflexes and the wonderfully sharp fruity aroma of the hibiscus.

## ESPUMA

This means foam and it can be made from any liquid you fancy. These foams enhance lots of recipes because they help provide an extra taste dimension. All you need is a cream syphon and 1–2 measuring spoons of xanthan or 1–2 egg whites depending on how firm the foam should be. Xanthan is a plant-based alginate and is used to thicken liquids. If you don't have a syphon you can also beat the liquid with xanthan in a bowl.

For foams prepared in a syphon always shake well before use and lather onto the drink. By following the recipe here you can froth up any fruit juice of your choice. The quantity of xanthan might have to be increased slightly.

## CREAMY ORANGE FOAM

Pour 500ml (16fl oz) fresh orange juice through a tea strainer so that the pulp doesn't clog up the syphon. Beat the juice with two measuring spoons of xanthan in a food processor for 5 seconds, then pour into the cream syphon, insert 1 nitrous oxide cartridge, and store in the fridge.

## GIN AND TONIC ESPUMA

Place 100ml (3½fl oz) gin, 150ml (5fl oz) tonic water, 50ml (1¾fl oz) lime juice, 30ml (1fl oz) sugar syrup, and 2 egg whites in a cream syphon. Insert 2 nitrous oxide cartridges and leave to rest in the fridge before use.

## BANANARUMA

Select a container that can be tightly sealed and pour in 1 bottle Anejo rum (700ml/ 1¼ pint), add 50g (1¾oz) dried banana chips and 30g (1oz) desiccated coconut, then leave to macerate at room temperature for 2 days. Open, strain, and decant into a clean bottle.

## SLOE GIN

Sloe gin is made by flavouring the gin with ripe sloes. The process of flavouring a cold liquid by putting in fruits, herbs, or spices is called maceration. The sloes should either be picked after the first frost or should be frozen initially for 1–2 days in the freezer. This lowers the water content and increases the sweetness in a similar way to grapes used for wine. Commercially produced sloe gin often has added sugar and colourings. By using my method you don't need any sugar – you can always sweeten it later in the drink. The only disadvantage of the natural maceration method is that the sloe gin oxidizes when exposed to light and oxygen, causing its colour to change week by week from a vivid blood red into a brownish red.

*Preparation:* Fill a clean bottle two-thirds full with sloes that you have either lightly pressed or pricked with a needle and pour in some good-quality gin. Leave in a cool place for 2–3 weeks, and from the second week check and test the gin. When the desired colour and intensity have been achieved, the gin can be filtered through a fine sieve and decanted into a new, impeccably clean, dark bottle. The aroma will be acidic and fruity.

## COLD DRIP

The cold dripper is a Japanese coffee machine for making cold brewed coffee (see p.12), which you can also use to produce highly aromatic alcoholic macerations without bitter substances. This is done by allowing a spirit, for example, gin, to drip through a filter of, for example, camomile flowers, hibiscus flowers, or nettles. For a 700ml (1¼ pint) bottle, this process takes around 24 hours. Below is my recipe for nettle cold drip (see p.132), which also works with other ingredients with some simple modifications.

## NETTLE COLD DRIP

Fill the filter chamber of a cold dripper with dried stinging nettle leaves. Scald the leaves in the filter chamber briefly with boiling water so that the maceration is a lovely green, rather than a brown, colour. Pour a bottle of Tanqueray No. Ten gin (700ml/1¼ pints) into the water tank and let it slowly drip through. Then decant into a clean bottle and store in the fridge. The cold drip will keep for several weeks, but will gradually turn darker and browner through oxidization and light exposure.

## BEETROOT COLD DRIP

Fill the filter chamber with dried beetroot chips and macerate with gin. You will find beetroot chips in specialist shops selling vegan products.

## HIBISCUS COLD DRIP

Place dried hibiscus flowers in the filter chamber and macerate with gin.

## AGAVE COFFEE

Place 80g (2¾oz) South American arabica coffee in the filter chamber of the cold dripper. Moisten with Tequila Reposado and pour the rest of the bottle into the water tank. Set the drip rate to 2 seconds per drop. Finally, sweeten with 20–40ml (¾–1¼fl oz) rock candy syrup (see p.160).

# ALCOHOL ABC

The list of types of alcohol and brands suitable for mixing is extensive, and the products you choose depends of course on your own individual taste. This glossary, therefore, is not a complete overview, but serves to complement the chapter "Basic alcoholic ingredients"(see pp.15–16) and is a list of recommendations for the alcoholic drinks that are used in the book.

### ABSINTHE

This herbal spirit is made with wormwood, anise, and fennel. For a long time it was suspected of triggering hallucinations, and as a result was even outlawed for many decades. Nowadays we know that no one is capable of drinking sufficient quantities to detect even the slightest hint of a hallucination. For drinking neat and mixing I love absinthes such as Duplais Verte, Blanche de Fougerolles, or François Guy.

### ALCHERMES

This is a bitter variety of liqueur from Italy, which along with alcohol typically contains sugar and spices such as cinnamon and cloves, but also cardamom, vanilla, and rose water, which lend it a quite unique sweetness. Campari also belongs to the family of alchermes. In Italy, where alchermes are popularly used in desserts such as zuppa romana, there are countless interesting small producers. These days the renowned crimson from the kermes scale insect, which was originally used to colour the beverage, has largely been replaced by artificial colouring. My own personal favourite is Luxardo Bitter.

### AMER PICON

A French bitter liqueur made from gentian and cinchona, which is over 200 years old. It has an alcohol content of 16% abv and a distinctive orange aroma. Picon bière is a top tip for summer, and not only in the south of France. Simply add a good shot of Picon to an ice-cold bitter ale and enjoy the warmth of summer.

### BITTERS

The most well known of these is the Angostura brand, established by German doctor Johann Gottlob Benjamin Siegert in the 1850s in Trinidad, a type of aromatic bitter that continues to be one of my favourites. My own Sexy Bitter and OK drops brands (see p.15) offer some interesting alternatives. Whichever brand, orange bitters are absolutely vital for lending a distinctive orange flavour to drinks. Over time, you should also acquire some special bitters such as lemon, grapefruit, and celery. I recommend the brand The Bitter Truth.

### BRANCA MENTA

An Italian bitter liqueur with an alcohol content of 38% abv and distinct peppermint notes. It is produced by the Fratelli Branca distillery, which is steeped in tradition and is even more renowned for its Fernet Branca. The two liqueurs differ only in the peppermint oil and sugar that are later added to the Branca Menta.

## CARPANO ANTICA FORMULA

This is a red wine-based vermouth made according to an old Carpano family recipe from 1786. This is my absolute top choice for classics such as the Manhattan or Martinez. Other red vermouths are also fun to mix with and of course every brand brings its own unique flavour characteristics to the drink.

## CHAMBORD

This French raspberry and blackberry liqueur with an alcohol content of 16.5% abv is characterized by its citrus and vanilla flavours.

## CHARTREUSE

A herbal liqueur that has been produced in the Grande Chartreuse monastery in the south east of France since 1737. Cast out by the French revolution and ultimately expropriated by the state, the silent monks kept their recipe secret until eventually they could once again produce this wonderfully intoxicating liqueur, made from more than one hundred herbs, in a location close to their old monastery. Only two monks at any time know the complete production process and so the recipe is passed down orally from generation to generation. Chartreuse verte is notorious for its high alcohol content of 55% abv; Chartreuse jeune is more harmonious and softer and the barrel aged V.E.P. qualities are a true joy for the palate.

## CHERRY HEERING

This cherry liqueur from the Danish brand Peter Heering is the oldest in the world and is distinguished from other varieties by its exceptional quality. It is deep red in colour and has an incredibly fruity aroma. Alternatively you could also use any other good dark red cherry liqueur.

## CHINA CHINA

A bitter liqueur from cinchona bark with zesty orange, herb, and caramel notes. For mixing I recommend the brand Bigallet.

## GINGER WINE

Ginger wine uses a centuries-old technique for extending the shelf life of white wine with the help of ginger, herbs, lemon zest, and sugar. The ginger notes are particularly prominent. Stone's ginger wine is a good-quality variety.

## LILLET

This is a French aperitif wine similar to vermouth. It's based on wines from Bordeaux, which are fortified and refined with fine herbs and citrus zest. Its characteristics are determined by the grapes used to make it; you can get Lillet in white, rosé, or red. The Lillet blanc and rosé are also suitable for drinking neat on the rocks or with tonic water as an aperitif. The red can be used in place of red vermouth in all my recipes.

## MARASCHINO

Luxardo Maraschino is the number one choice among bartenders across the globe: a clear cherry liqueur from Marasca cherries, which is an indispensable ingredient for many drinks. Even when used in minimal quantities, a dash of maraschino is a marvellous thing. According to my colleague Andrew Nicholls from Amsterdam, it is "the Jedi power of the bartender, but you must know how to use it".

## MOZART DRY

The renowned Mozart distillery in Salzburg produces this dry cocoa or chocolate distillate. Adequate alternatives can sometimes be found from certain other fruit distillers.

## NOILLY PRAT

A dry French white wine, which is macerated with herbs and stored in oak barrels for a year. Available since 1857 in the USA, Noilly Prat has accompanied the cocktail story over the years and certain classic recipes are inconceivable without it.

## FRUIT BRANDY

The difference between good quality and poor quality is particularly noticeable in fruit brandies, even when mixing. Anyone who has ever tried Hans Reisetbauer or Christoph Keller's brandies won't be taken in so easily again. Good brandies don't smell of alcohol, but rather of the fruit used in the distilling process, and are therefore infinitely superior to spirits. In fruit brandies the initial product is mashed, fermented, and subsequently distilled, whereas with spirits you often have a lower-quality distillate based on a neutral alcohol, which merely absorbs the fruit flavour.

## ORANGE CURAÇAO

This is a liqueur based on orange zest. The best choice is Ferrand Dry Orange Curaçao. Other good products include Grand Marnier, Cointreau or triple sec with a good-quality provenance.

## ORANGE BLOSSOM WATER

Drinks can be imbued with a floral fragrance by using this alcohol-free essence of orange blossom. Available from the brand The Bitter Truth or from some supermarkets.

## PIMENTO DRAM

This rum liqueur from the Caribbean, with its aromas of nutmeg, cinnamon, cloves, and a distinctive allspice flavour, is commonly used particularly in tiki recipes. The Bitter Truth supplies a very fine Pimento dram.

## PORT

This fortified wine from Portugal is matured in barrels. Ordinary vintages should be drunk young (ruby) and after a short storage in a large oak barrel are known as "tawny". Better vintages are matured over many years in smaller barrels (Colheita, old tawny) or in the bottle like the LBV (late bottled vintage). Exceptional vintages don't hit the shops as vintage port for at least 10 years and often only reach their peak after decades in the bottle.

## SAKE

Japanese sake is neither a beer nor a wine. Sake is made by fermenting mashed and fermented rice to produce alcohol. If no additional ingredients are added after fine filtering, the sake is designated Junmai (just rice). If things are helped along a bit with some alcohol, the sake is referred to as Honjozo. The quality of the sake depends on the degree to which the rice grains are polished because the exterior contains many intrusive flavours, oils, and proteins. The additional endorsement Ginjo in the name indicates that at least 40 per cent of the rice grain was polished off beforehand. With Daiginjo sake the figure is at least 50 per cent. Good sake should be enjoyed chilled in a lovely white wine glass and never drunk warmer than body temperature. Boiling hot sake is a faux pas; it makes dry qualities sweet and destroys all the flavours.

## SHOCHU

Also from Japan, this is often mentioned in the same breath as sake, even though it is actually completely different: namely a simple brandy with an alcohol content of around 25% abv. It can be produced from anything containing starch – from chestnuts to sesame seeds. Cheaper varieties of the drink are usually distilled from beets or sweet potatoes.

## TIA MARIA

This Jamaican rum-based coffee liqueur can be readily used if you don't fancy making your own agave coffee (see p.163).

## GIFFARD VANILLE DE MADAGASCAR

A good choice of vanilla liqueur. Alternatively other brands can also be used.

## VERMOUTH AND WINE APERITIFS

My recommendations can be found with the relevant individual brands. Once opened, all vermouths, wine aperitifs, and also port should be kept in a cool, dark place. All these drinks are based on wine, which is given a longer shelf life thanks to alcohol, barks, and herbs, but these are perishable once the bottle is open.

## VODKA

Vodka is indispensable as a base for many long drinks, such as the Moscow Mule. It is generally neutral tasting and lends itself as an option to those who drink for the effect rather than on account of the taste. In addition, it is a good basis for macerations and bitters and is suitable for making syrups, which tend to keep well.

## YUZU SAKE

Yuzu is a small and highly aromatic lime variety from Japan. It is a sort of Japanese equivalent to Italian limoncello: just as delicately sweet, but far more aromatic.

# DRINKS BY ALCOHOLIC BASE

## CHAMPAGNE

| | |
|---|---|
| Caramellow Royal | 132 |
| Champagne Cocktail | 80 |
| Cold Duck 2011 | 74 |
| Golden Champagne | 30 |
| Haus der Kunst Cocktail | 120 |
| Mr Serious Champagne Cocktail | 38 |
| My Buck and Breck | 130 |
| Nettle Tea | 132 |
| Royal Camomile Tea | 122 |
| Two Hundred | 144 |

## COGNAC

| | |
|---|---|
| Arpi Gardenia | 140 |
| French Daisy | 86 |
| My Buck and Breck | 130 |
| Vanilla Punch | 96 |

## GIN

| | |
|---|---|
| Beetroot Gimlet | 124 |
| Dry Martini | 76 |
| *Frozen Gin and Tonic* | *82* |
| Gintelligence No. 1 | 36 |
| Gintelligence No. 2 | 142 |
| Golden Bramble | 54 |
| Golden Bartini on the Rocks | 78 |
| Haus der Kunst Cocktail | 120 |
| *London Buck* | *44* |
| Pink Gin No. Ten | 84 |
| Royal Hibiscus Gin Fizz | 136 |
| Yamahai | 60 |

## LIQUEUR

| | |
|---|---|
| Bishop | 50 |
| Blood and Sand | 128 |
| Chocolate Cocktail | 114 |
| Pharmacy | 140 |
| Rescue Remedy Punch | 50 |
| Walther PPK | 66 |
| Yellow Smash | 108 |

## FRUIT BRANDY

| | |
|---|---|
| Old McCarthy | 98 |
| Plum Fizz | 32 |
| Williams Sour | 32 |

## PORT

| | |
|---|---|
| Chocolate Cocktail | 114 |
| Suburbia | 148 |

## RUM

| | |
|---|---|
| Banksy | 48 |
| Captain Strainer's Plantation Punch | 150 |
| Corn 'n' Oil | 100 |
| Crustafarai | 104 |
| *Dark & Stormy* | *44* |
| Hot Buttered Coconut Rum | 138 |
| Klaus of Pain | 58 |
| Lemmy Kilmister's Rum Grog | 62 |
| *Petit Punch* | *100* |
| Raspberry Rum Smash | 110 |
| Rasta Nail | 106 |
| Royal Camomile Tea | 122 |

The drinks in italics appear as a recipe described within another recipe.

# DRINKS BY OCCASION

**FOR LOTS OF GUESTS...**

**... AS A WELCOME**

| | |
|---|---|
| Caramellow Royal | 132 |
| Champagne Cocktail | 80 |
| Dry Martini | 76 |
| East Village | 52 |
| Golden Bartini on the Rocks | 78 |
| Golden Champagne | 30 |
| Mr Serious Champagne Cocktail | 38 |
| Nettle Tea | 132 |
| Old McCarthy | 98 |

**...FOR A LONG SUMMER NIGHT**

| | |
|---|---|
| *Americano* | *146* |
| Captain Strainer's Plantation Punch | 150 |
| *Dark and Stormy* | *44* |
| Fresh Paloma | 64 |
| *Frozen Gin and Tonic* | *82* |
| Frozen Sazerac | 82 |
| *Frozen Vermouth and Tonic* | *82* |
| Ginger Beer | 42 |
| Golden Bartini on the Rocks | 78 |
| Klaus of Pain | 58 |
| *London Buck* | *44* |
| Moscow Mule | 44 |

**WARM AND SOOTHING**

| | |
|---|---|
| Bishop | 50 |
| Gintelligence No. 1 | 36 |
| Gintelligence No. 2 | 142 |
| Hot Buttered Coconut Rum | 138 |
| Lemmy Kilmister's Rum Grog | 62 |
| Rescue Remedy Punch | 50 |
| Samurai Spirit | 40 |

**ENJOYMENT WITHOUT ALCOHOL**

| | |
|---|---|
| Arshavin | 68 |
| Bitterman's Friend | 68 |
| Ginger Beer | 42 |
| Munich Iced Coffee | 70 |
| Santino | 46 |
| *Sexy Ginger Beer* | *44* |
| Toxic Garden | 56 |

*The drinks in italics appear as a recipe described within another recipe.*

# SUPPLY SOURCES

Bar accessories and most of the ingredients listed in the book can be obtained from specialist shops and well-stocked drinks retailers. If you have no joy finding something locally you can always turn to online retailers. The following sites are recommended:

**BAR ACCESSORIES:**
www.cocktailkingdom.com

**COFFEE, COLD DRIPPERS AND ACCESSORIES:**
www.coffeehit.co.uk

**JR COCKTAIL SHAKERS:**
www.jr-shaker.com

**ABSINTHE, MEZCAL, SPIRITS:**
www.thewhiskyexchange.com
www.gerrys.uk.com

**SEXY BITTERS, OK DROPS:**
www.lion-spirits.de

**GOLDEN MONACO EXTRA DRY TONIC WATER AND SOFT DRINKS:**
www.aquamonaco.com

**SAKE AND JAPANESE INGREDIENTS:**
www.japan-gourmet.com

# THE AUTHOR & THE PHOTOGRAPHER

**KLAUS ST. RAINER**
is one of the best known and most successful bartenders in Germany. He has been involved in gastronomy since 1986 and worked for five years as head barman for Ernst Lechthaler before he transferred over to the legendary Schumann's Bar in Munich for seven years. In 2010 he opened the Golden Bar in Munich's Haus der Kunst together with Leonie von Carnap. In 2012 he was awarded "Bartender of the Year" at the Mixology Bar Awards, and in 2013 his bar achieved the distinction of "Bar of the Year". The British magazine *Drinks International* rated the Golden Bar one of the "Top 50 Bars of the World".
Klaus St. Rainer is an adjudicator in many international competitions and runs training sessions all around the world. In addition, he is a co-founder of the Munich Bar Circle (Barzirkel München), proprietor of a cocktail shaker manufacturer, and sells his own bitters and tonic water.

**WWW.GOLDENEBAR.DE**

**ARMIN SMAILOVIC**
is one of the most prestigious portrait photographers and photojournalists in Germany. Since 1995 he has worked as a freelance photographer around the globe for German and international magazines. He has won multiple awards. Among other things he won the LEAD Award's 2010 "best coverage of the year" and 2013 "best portrait photography of the year" and in 2014 received the highly regarded Hansel Mieth prize. Since 2010 he has been a founding member of the Munich FotoDoks festival for documentary photography. He lives in Munich and Sarajevo.

# AUTHOR'S THANKS

Thank you to Leonie and my family, in which I also include my Screw Crew: Oliver von Carnap, Maximilian Hildebrandt, Claudius Kramer Brudnjak, Robbie Flörke, Jenny Lang, Mirko Hecktor, Julia Nather, Wicked, Ali, Anton Utin, Julian Zerressen, Dennis Richter, Chrissla Rieder, Messi Messerklinger, Ervin Mesanovic, Arpad Nikhazi, Axa Hötzinger, Ina Chil Soon Leuther, Wilfried Scherbinek, Christian Kaul, Jürgen Wiese, Julian Kerkoff, Gsölli Gsöllpointner, Giaco Giambo and all the other fine people who have worked and continue to work with us. Particular thanks must also go Julia Otterbach and my close friend Armin Smailovic for their fantastic collaboration on this book.

**Text** Klaus St Rainer
**Photography** Armin Smailovic

**For DK Germany**
**Editor** Ulrike Goldstein
**Design & Typography** Julia Otterbach
**Repro** Farbsatz, Neuried/Munich
**Publisher** Monika Schlitzer
**Project Support** Andrea Göppner
**Production Manager** Dorothee Whittaker
**Production Coordinator** Madlen Richter
**Production** Kim Weghorn

**For DK UK**
**Translator** Alison Tunley
**Editor** Claire Cross
**Project Editor** Kathryn Meeker
**Senior Art Editor** Glenda Fisher
**Producer, Pre-Production** Tony Phipps
**Producer** Stephanie McConnell
**Creative Technical Support** Sonia Charbonnier
**Managing Editor** Stephanie Farrow
**Managing Art Editor** Christine Keilty

First published in Great Britain in 2016 by
Dorling Kindersley Limited
80 Strand, London, WC2R 0RL

Copyright © 2016 Dorling Kindersley Limited
Translation copyright © Dorling Kindersley Limited, 2016
A Penguin Random House Company
10 9 8 7 6 5 4 3
005–294011–Nov/2016

A CIP catalogue record for this book
is available from the British Library.
ISBN: 978-0-2412-5563-6

Printed and bound in China.

All images © Dorling Kindersley Limited
For further information see: www.dkimages.com

A WORLD OF IDEAS:
SEE ALL THERE IS TO KNOW

**www.dk.com**